Bio-Based Solutions for Climate Change: Reducing Emissions with Bio-Based Technologies While Building Resilience Enhancing Carbon Sequestration and Restoring Ecosystems

Copyright

Bio-Based Solutions for Climate Change: Reducing Emissions with Bio-Based Technologies While Building Resilience Enhancing Carbon Sequestration and Restoring Ecosystems

© 2025 Robert C. Brears

ISBN (eBook): 978-1-991369-87-1

ISBN (Paperback): 978-1-991369-88-8

Published by Global Climate Solutions

First Edition, 2025

Cover design and interior layout by Global Climate Solutions

Table of Contents

Introduction

Bio-based solutions leverage natural systems and biological resources to address environmental challenges while promoting sustainability. These solutions utilize renewable biological materials—such as plants, microorganisms, and bioengineered compounds—to mitigate carbon emissions, restore ecosystems, and enhance land management practices. They contribute to carbon sequestration by enhancing soil health, increasing vegetation cover, and improving biodiversity. Additionally, bio-based products, including biofuels, bioplastics, and biochar, offer alternatives to fossil-based materials, reducing dependence on finite resources.

Beyond their environmental benefits, bio-based solutions play a crucial role in circular economy models by minimizing waste and promoting resource efficiency. They integrate well with existing sustainability strategies, including regenerative agriculture, ecosystem restoration, and nature-based solutions. By fostering synergy between biological processes and technological advancements, bio-based approaches provide scalable opportunities for industries and policymakers seeking to implement effective climate action. However, their widespread adoption depends on innovation, supportive policies, and targeted financial mechanisms to drive progress.

Introduction to Key Themes

This book explores how bio-based solutions contribute to emissions reduction, ecosystem restoration, and sustainable land management through the lenses of technology, finance, governance, and innovation. These four pillars are critical for understanding the potential and challenges of integrating bio-based approaches into mainstream climate strategies.

Technological advancements enhance the efficiency and scalability of bio-based solutions, from biochar and microbial soil enhancements to synthetic biology and bioremediation. Financial mechanisms, including green bonds, carbon markets, and impact investing, determine the feasibility of large-scale implementation. Governance frameworks, encompassing regulations, policies, and incentives, shape the integration of bio-based solutions into national and global sustainability agendas. Finally, innovation drives continuous improvement, ensuring that bio-based strategies remain effective and adaptable in a changing climate.

By examining these dimensions, this book provides a comprehensive perspective on how bio-based solutions can support long-term sustainability and resilience while addressing critical environmental challenges.

Importance for Climate Action

Addressing climate change requires multifaceted approaches that integrate emissions reduction with ecosystem restoration and sustainable land management. Bio-based solutions play a pivotal role in this effort by leveraging natural carbon sinks, enhancing biodiversity, and reducing reliance on fossil-based resources. Unlike conventional mitigation strategies, bio-based approaches offer co-benefits, including soil regeneration, water conservation, and improved agricultural productivity.

As global emissions continue to rise, industries and policymakers are increasingly looking for scalable, nature-driven solutions. Bio-based technologies, such as algae-based carbon capture, biochar applications, and bioplastics, provide tangible pathways to reducing greenhouse gas emissions while promoting a circular economy. Moreover, regenerative land management practices, including agroforestry and restorative agriculture, enhance carbon sequestration and ecosystem resilience.

However, the transition to a bio-based economy requires coordinated action across multiple sectors. Effective policies, financial investments, and technological advancements are essential to overcoming barriers to adoption. This book aims to highlight the pathways for integrating bio-based solutions into climate action strategies, demonstrating their potential to accelerate sustainability transitions. By fostering collaboration among governments, businesses, and researchers, bio-based solutions can drive meaningful progress in the fight against climate change while ensuring long-term environmental and economic stability.

Chapter 1: The Science Behind Bio-Based Solutions

Bio-based solutions harness biological processes and natural systems to address climate change, restore ecosystems, and promote sustainable land management. Rooted in the principles of ecology, these solutions rely on the ability of living organisms—such as plants, microbes, and fungi—to sequester carbon, regenerate soils, and enhance biodiversity. Understanding the science behind these mechanisms is essential for optimizing their effectiveness and integrating them into broader sustainability strategies.

This chapter explores the fundamental scientific principles that underpin bio-based solutions, including photosynthesis, soil carbon storage, nutrient cycling, and microbial activity. It examines how these processes contribute to emissions reduction and environmental resilience. Additionally, it highlights the interactions between biological and physical systems, emphasizing the importance of maintaining ecosystem balance to maximize climate benefits.

By providing a scientific foundation for bio-based approaches, this chapter sets the stage for subsequent discussions on technology, finance, governance, and innovation.

Definition and Scope of Bio-Based Solutions

Bio-based solutions refer to strategies that leverage biological processes, renewable natural resources, and living organisms to address environmental challenges such as climate change, land degradation, and biodiversity loss. These solutions utilize biological materials—including plants, microorganisms, fungi, and algae—to develop sustainable alternatives to conventional, fossil-based products and processes. Bio-based solutions encompass a wide range of applications, from carbon sequestration and soil restoration to bioenergy production and biodegradable materials.

A core principle of bio-based solutions is their reliance on renewable biological resources rather than non-renewable inputs. This approach promotes circularity, reducing waste while enhancing ecosystem functions. For example, biochar—produced from biomass—improves soil health and increases carbon sequestration, while algae-based carbon capture systems absorb atmospheric CO_2 and generate valuable bioproducts. Similarly, bioengineered crops can enhance soil carbon storage and reduce synthetic fertilizer dependence, supporting more sustainable agricultural practices.

Bio-based solutions contribute to climate mitigation by removing carbon dioxide from the atmosphere and storing it in vegetation, soils, and biomass-based materials. They also enhance adaptation by strengthening ecosystem resilience against climate impacts such as extreme weather events, soil erosion, and water scarcity. For instance, regenerative agriculture—incorporating cover crops, no-till farming, and agroforestry—enhances soil fertility, reduces emissions, and conserves water.

The scope of bio-based solutions extends across multiple sectors, including agriculture, forestry, industry, and urban development. In agriculture, bio-based fertilizers and pest control methods replace synthetic chemicals, reducing environmental harm. In forestry, afforestation and reforestation initiatives enhance carbon storage and biodiversity. In industry, bio-based plastics, textiles, and construction materials provide sustainable alternatives to petroleum-based products. In urban settings, green infrastructure—such as bioengineered wetlands and living roofs—improves air quality, reduces urban heat, and manages stormwater.

Despite their potential, bio-based solutions face challenges related to scalability, cost, and policy integration. Ensuring their effectiveness requires a combination of scientific research, technological advancements, financial investment, and supportive governance frameworks. As industries and policymakers seek sustainable pathways to reduce emissions and restore ecosystems, bio-based solutions offer a critical tool for achieving global climate goals.

By understanding the definition and scope of bio-based solutions, stakeholders can better integrate them into broader sustainability strategies, fostering a shift toward nature-positive economies. The following sections will explore the scientific mechanisms that drive bio-based approaches, highlighting their role in emissions reduction, ecosystem restoration, and sustainable land management.

Role of Biological Systems in Carbon Sequestration and Biodiversity

Biological systems play a crucial role in carbon sequestration and biodiversity enhancement, forming the foundation of bio-based solutions for climate action. Natural ecosystems, including forests, wetlands, grasslands, and agricultural lands, act as carbon sinks by absorbing and storing atmospheric carbon dioxide (CO_2) in biomass and soils. At the same time, these ecosystems support biodiversity by providing habitats for a vast array of plant, animal, and microbial species. Understanding the processes through which biological systems sequester carbon and maintain biodiversity is essential for developing effective strategies to combat climate change and ecosystem degradation.

Carbon Sequestration in Terrestrial Ecosystems

Terrestrial ecosystems contribute significantly to carbon sequestration through vegetation growth and soil carbon storage. Plants absorb CO_2 from the atmosphere through photosynthesis, converting it into organic matter that is stored in leaves, stems, and roots. Forests are particularly effective at sequestering carbon, with tropical rainforests, temperate forests, and boreal forests collectively storing vast amounts of carbon in biomass and soil. Afforestation, reforestation, and improved forest management practices enhance this natural carbon sink, increasing long-term sequestration potential.

Soils also play a critical role in carbon sequestration. Organic matter derived from plant material, root exudates, and microbial activity contributes to soil carbon pools. Regenerative agricultural practices, such as cover cropping, no-till farming, and rotational grazing, improve soil health and increase carbon storage. Biochar application—produced from biomass pyrolysis—further enhances soil carbon sequestration by stabilizing organic matter and improving soil structure. These strategies not only sequester carbon but also enhance soil fertility and resilience to climate variability.

Carbon Sequestration in Aquatic Ecosystems

Aquatic ecosystems, including mangroves, seagrasses, and salt marshes, provide significant carbon storage through "blue carbon" sequestration. These coastal and marine habitats absorb CO_2 and store carbon in sediment layers for centuries. Mangrove forests, for example, trap organic material in anaerobic soils, preventing its decomposition and release of CO_2. Seagrass meadows and salt marshes function similarly, capturing carbon through root structures and sediment deposition.

Conserving and restoring blue carbon ecosystems is essential for maintaining their sequestration potential. However, these ecosystems are increasingly threatened by coastal development, pollution, and climate change. Effective management, including marine protected areas and sustainable aquaculture practices, can help safeguard their role as carbon sinks while promoting biodiversity.

Biodiversity Enhancement and Ecosystem Resilience

Biodiversity plays an integral role in the stability and function of ecosystems. Diverse ecosystems are more resilient to environmental stressors, such as extreme weather events, invasive species, and disease outbreaks. Higher species diversity enhances ecosystem productivity, improves nutrient cycling, and increases carbon sequestration capacity.

Forests, wetlands, and grasslands with high biodiversity support complex interactions between plants, animals, and microbes. Mycorrhizal fungi, for instance, form symbiotic relationships with plant roots, enhancing nutrient uptake and promoting carbon storage in soils. Pollinators, including bees and butterflies, contribute to plant reproduction and genetic diversity, ensuring the resilience of natural ecosystems.

In agricultural landscapes, biodiversity-friendly practices—such as agroforestry, intercropping, and conservation buffers—support pollinators, beneficial insects, and soil microorganisms. These practices not only enhance biodiversity but also improve soil health, water retention, and crop resilience. Integrating biodiversity conservation into land-use planning strengthens the adaptive capacity of ecosystems while maintaining their carbon sequestration functions.

Interconnected Benefits of Carbon Sequestration and Biodiversity

The relationship between carbon sequestration and biodiversity is mutually reinforcing. Healthy, biodiverse ecosystems sequester more carbon, while carbon-rich environments support diverse species assemblages. Protecting and restoring natural ecosystems, therefore, provides co-benefits for climate mitigation and ecological stability.

However, habitat destruction, deforestation, and unsustainable land use threaten these natural processes. Implementing bio-based solutions—such as reforestation, soil regeneration, and blue carbon conservation—requires coordinated efforts between policymakers, industries, and local communities. Financial incentives, regulatory frameworks, and technological advancements play a vital role in scaling these solutions.

By leveraging biological systems for carbon sequestration and biodiversity enhancement, bio-based strategies can address multiple environmental challenges simultaneously. The next section explores the mechanisms underlying these processes, including photosynthesis, nutrient cycling, and microbial activity, to provide a deeper understanding of how bio-based solutions function at the scientific level.

Mechanisms: Photosynthesis, Soil Carbon Storage, and Nutrient Cycling

Bio-based solutions rely on fundamental biological mechanisms that drive carbon sequestration and ecosystem stability. Among these, photosynthesis, soil carbon storage, and nutrient cycling are the most significant processes enabling the capture and retention of atmospheric carbon while maintaining soil health and ecosystem resilience. Understanding how these mechanisms function provides a scientific basis for optimizing bio-based strategies for climate mitigation and sustainable land management.

Photosynthesis and Carbon Capture

Photosynthesis is the primary process through which plants, algae, and certain bacteria capture atmospheric CO_2 and convert it into organic matter. Through this process, solar energy is used to synthesize glucose from CO_2 and water, releasing oxygen as a byproduct.

This fundamental biological process underpins the global carbon cycle, serving as the initial step in carbon sequestration. Terrestrial plants store carbon in their biomass—leaves, stems, and roots—while aquatic plants, including phytoplankton, play a crucial role in marine carbon sequestration. Fast-growing plant species, such as bamboo and algae, have particularly high carbon capture efficiency, making them valuable for bio-based climate solutions.

Maximizing photosynthetic efficiency through afforestation, reforestation, and improved crop varieties enhances carbon capture potential. Additionally, sustainable land-use practices, such as agroforestry and rotational planting, can maintain high photosynthetic activity while supporting biodiversity and soil health.

Soil Carbon Storage and Sequestration

Soils serve as one of the largest carbon sinks on the planet, storing more carbon than the atmosphere and all vegetation combined. Carbon enters the soil primarily through plant residues, root exudates, and microbial activity. Once incorporated, organic carbon undergoes decomposition, with a portion becoming stabilized in long-term storage as soil organic matter (SOM). This stored carbon contributes to soil fertility, water retention, and overall ecosystem resilience.

Soil carbon sequestration can be enhanced through regenerative agricultural practices such as:

- **No-till farming**: Reduces soil disturbance, preserving organic matter and microbial activity.
- **Cover cropping**: Introduces diverse plant species that increase organic inputs into the soil.
- **Composting and biochar application**: Improves soil structure while enhancing carbon stabilization.
- **Restorative grazing**: Ensures balanced nutrient cycling and organic matter retention.

However, soil carbon storage is sensitive to land degradation, deforestation, and intensive farming. Unsustainable practices can deplete soil organic matter, releasing stored carbon back into the atmosphere. Preventing soil erosion, maintaining vegetation cover, and restoring degraded lands are critical for maximizing soil carbon sequestration.

Nutrient Cycling and Ecosystem Stability

Nutrient cycling refers to the movement of essential elements—such as carbon, nitrogen, and phosphorus—through the soil, plants, and microbial communities. This process maintains ecosystem productivity and ensures that carbon sequestration mechanisms remain efficient over time.

Key Components of Nutrient Cycling:

1. Decomposition and Organic Matter Breakdown

    1. Dead plant material and organic waste are decomposed by microbes, fungi, and detritivores.
    2. This process releases nutrients back into the soil, making them available for plant uptake.

2. Nitrogen Fixation and Carbon Storage

    1. Certain bacteria, such as Rhizobia in legume root nodules, convert atmospheric nitrogen (N_2) into plant-usable forms.
    2. This biological nitrogen fixation enhances soil fertility, reducing the need for synthetic fertilizers that contribute to emissions.

3. Mycorrhizal Associations

    1. Symbiotic fungi enhance plant nutrient absorption by extending root networks.
    2. These interactions facilitate carbon transfer between plants and soil, improving sequestration potential.

By maintaining efficient nutrient cycling, bio-based solutions support ecosystem resilience, ensuring that carbon remains stored in plants and soils for extended periods. Sustainable land management practices, including organic farming, rewilding, and wetland conservation, play a vital role in preserving these natural cycles.

Synergies with Conventional Sustainability Strategies

Bio-based solutions align with and enhance conventional sustainability strategies, creating integrated approaches to climate action, ecosystem restoration, and sustainable land management. By leveraging natural processes, bio-based solutions complement existing sustainability initiatives, including circular economy models, renewable energy transitions, sustainable agriculture, and urban green infrastructure. These synergies maximize environmental benefits while improving efficiency and long-term resilience.

Integration with the Circular Economy

The circular economy aims to minimize waste and optimize resource use by designing systems that reuse, recycle, and regenerate materials. Bio-based solutions naturally support circularity by reducing reliance on fossil-based products and creating regenerative systems. For example, biodegradable bio-based plastics reduce plastic pollution and return organic matter to the environment without persistent waste. Similarly, biochar production from agricultural residues enhances soil fertility while sequestering carbon, closing the loop between waste management and land restoration.

Additionally, bio-based materials such as algae-derived biopolymers and fungal-based packaging offer sustainable alternatives to petrochemical products, aligning with circular economy principles. By replacing non-renewable materials with biodegradable, carbon-neutral alternatives, bio-based solutions contribute to a more sustainable production and consumption model.

Enhancing Renewable Energy and Decarbonization Efforts

The transition to renewable energy sources is a cornerstone of climate mitigation. Bio-based solutions complement this shift by providing sustainable biomass energy, biofuels, and biohydrogen. Unlike fossil fuels, bioenergy sources derived from crop residues, algae, and organic waste can be carbon-neutral or even carbon-negative when integrated with carbon capture and storage technologies.

For example, advanced biofuels—such as cellulosic ethanol and algae-based biodiesel—reduce greenhouse gas emissions compared to conventional fossil fuels. When used in combination with solar, wind, and hydroelectric power, bioenergy diversifies renewable energy portfolios, ensuring energy security while reducing emissions. Moreover, anaerobic digestion of organic waste generates biogas, a renewable energy source that can replace natural gas in heating and electricity generation.

Supporting Sustainable Agriculture and Food Systems

Conventional agricultural sustainability strategies aim to enhance productivity while minimizing environmental impacts. Bio-based solutions reinforce these goals by improving soil health, reducing dependence on synthetic fertilizers, and enhancing water retention. Practices such as agroforestry, cover cropping, and regenerative grazing integrate bio-based principles to increase carbon sequestration and biodiversity within agricultural landscapes.

Bio-based fertilizers, including compost and microbial inoculants, enhance soil fertility without the harmful effects of synthetic nitrogen fertilizers, which contribute to greenhouse gas emissions and water pollution. Furthermore, bio-based pest control solutions, such as microbial biopesticides, support integrated pest management strategies, reducing chemical pesticide use while preserving ecosystem balance.

Strengthening Urban Sustainability and Green Infrastructure

Cities increasingly incorporate green infrastructure to mitigate climate impacts, enhance biodiversity, and improve air and water quality. Bio-based solutions align with these efforts by providing nature-based approaches to urban resilience. Living roofs, constructed wetlands, and tree-lined corridors enhance carbon sequestration while reducing urban heat effects.

Moreover, bioengineered solutions, such as algae-based air filtration systems and microbial wastewater treatment technologies, provide sustainable alternatives to conventional urban infrastructure. By integrating bio-based materials into building design and stormwater management, cities can create regenerative environments that support climate adaptation and sustainability.

Chapter 2: Bio-Based Technologies for Emissions Reduction

Reducing greenhouse gas emissions is a central objective of global climate action, and bio-based technologies offer innovative pathways to achieving this goal. These technologies harness biological processes and renewable materials to capture carbon, replace fossil-based products, and improve resource efficiency across industries. By integrating scientific advancements with nature-driven approaches, bio-based solutions provide scalable alternatives that contribute to a low-carbon economy.

This chapter explores key bio-based technologies that support emissions reduction, including biochar for soil carbon sequestration, algae-based carbon capture, bioengineered crops, and biodegradable materials. It examines how these innovations can be implemented across sectors such as agriculture, energy, and manufacturing to lower emissions while enhancing sustainability. Additionally, it discusses the challenges and opportunities associated with scaling bio-based technologies, highlighting their role in transitioning to a more resilient and climate-friendly future.

Overview of Bio-Based Technologies

Bio-based technologies leverage biological processes and renewable materials to reduce greenhouse gas emissions, enhance carbon sequestration, and replace fossil-based products. These technologies span multiple sectors, including agriculture, energy, industry, and waste management, offering scalable solutions to mitigate climate change while promoting sustainability. By utilizing natural systems, bio-based technologies help create circular and regenerative approaches to resource use, minimizing environmental impact.

One of the key areas of bio-based technology development is carbon sequestration. Biochar, produced through the pyrolysis of biomass, enhances soil carbon storage while improving soil fertility and water retention. Algae-based carbon capture systems absorb atmospheric CO_2 efficiently, with applications in biofuel production, bioplastics, and wastewater treatment. These technologies offer nature-based solutions to reduce emissions while providing valuable byproducts for agriculture and industry.

Bioengineered crops and soil microbes are another area of innovation. Advanced plant breeding and genetic modification improve carbon uptake, soil health, and resilience to climate stressors. Microbial inoculants, including nitrogen-fixing bacteria and mycorrhizal fungi, reduce the need for synthetic fertilizers, decreasing emissions associated with nitrogen production and application. These approaches contribute to more sustainable agricultural systems that enhance productivity while reducing environmental impact.

The development of bio-based materials offers alternatives to petroleum-based products that contribute to carbon emissions. Bioplastics, derived from sources such as corn, sugarcane, and algae, provide biodegradable alternatives to conventional plastics, reducing pollution and fossil fuel dependency. Bio-based construction materials, including mycelium-based composites and engineered wood, offer sustainable building solutions with lower carbon footprints. These materials align with circular economy principles, reducing waste while sequestering carbon in long-lasting products.

In the energy sector, biofuels such as biodiesel, bioethanol, and biohydrogen provide renewable alternatives to fossil fuels. These fuels, produced from biomass, algae, and organic waste, offer lower emissions and can be integrated into existing energy infrastructures. Advances in second- and third-generation biofuels focus on maximizing efficiency while minimizing competition with food production and land use.

Despite their potential, scaling bio-based technologies requires investment, supportive policies, and infrastructure development. Addressing barriers such as cost, production efficiency, and regulatory challenges will be essential to integrating bio-based solutions into mainstream sustainability strategies. As industries and governments seek alternatives to traditional emissions-intensive processes, bio-based technologies offer a viable path toward reducing environmental impact while promoting long-term sustainability.

Biochar and Soil Carbon Sequestration

Biochar is a carbon-rich material produced through the pyrolysis of biomass under low-oxygen conditions. This process converts organic matter—such as agricultural residues, wood waste, and manure—into a stable form of carbon that can be applied to soils to enhance carbon sequestration, improve soil fertility, and reduce greenhouse gas emissions. By storing carbon in a solid, long-lasting form, biochar serves as an effective strategy for mitigating climate change while supporting sustainable land management practices.

The Role of Biochar in Carbon Sequestration

One of the primary benefits of biochar is its ability to store carbon for centuries or even millennia. Unlike organic matter that decomposes and releases CO_2 back into the atmosphere, biochar remains stable in the soil, preventing carbon from re-entering the carbon cycle. This makes biochar a reliable method for long-term carbon sequestration. Estimates suggest that large-scale biochar application could remove significant amounts of CO_2 from the atmosphere, complementing other emissions reduction strategies.

Additionally, biochar contributes to reduced methane (CH_4) and nitrous oxide (N_2O) emissions from soils. These greenhouse gases have a higher global warming potential than CO_2, making their reduction crucial for climate mitigation. Biochar alters soil microbial communities and nutrient availability, leading to lower emissions of these potent gases.

Soil Health Benefits of Biochar

Beyond its role in carbon sequestration, biochar improves soil structure, water retention, and nutrient availability. Its porous structure enhances soil aeration and microbial activity, creating optimal conditions for plant growth. This is particularly beneficial in degraded or nutrient-poor soils, where biochar application can restore fertility and increase agricultural productivity.

Biochar also enhances water-holding capacity, reducing irrigation needs and improving resilience to drought. In sandy soils, it prevents excessive water drainage, while in clay soils, it enhances permeability and prevents compaction. By improving soil water retention, biochar contributes to sustainable agriculture and reduces pressure on water resources.

Biochar and Circular Economy Practices

The production of biochar aligns with circular economy principles by repurposing agricultural and forestry waste. Instead of allowing biomass to decay and release CO_2, converting it into biochar provides a sustainable way to manage organic waste while delivering climate benefits. Biochar can also be integrated into composting processes, further enhancing nutrient cycling and organic matter stabilization.

Challenges and Future Prospects

Despite its potential, scaling biochar application faces challenges related to production costs, consistency in quality, and policy support. Large-scale adoption requires infrastructure for biomass collection, pyrolysis facilities, and financial incentives for landowners and farmers. Research continues to explore ways to optimize biochar production methods and integrate it into climate policies, such as carbon markets and sustainable agriculture programs.

By improving soil carbon sequestration, reducing emissions, and enhancing soil health, biochar represents a valuable tool for addressing climate change. Its integration into agricultural and land management practices can provide long-term environmental and economic benefits, supporting global efforts to transition toward more sustainable systems.

Algae-Based Carbon Capture

Algae-based carbon capture is an innovative bio-based solution that utilizes microalgae and macroalgae to absorb and store atmospheric CO_2. Algae, like all photosynthetic organisms, convert CO_2 into organic biomass through photosynthesis. However, their rapid growth rate, high efficiency in carbon uptake, and ability to thrive in diverse environments make them particularly effective for large-scale carbon sequestration. This process offers a natural and scalable way to reduce greenhouse gas emissions while generating valuable byproducts for various industries.

How Algae Capture Carbon

Microalgae, such as Chlorella and Spirulina, and macroalgae, such as kelp and seaweed, absorb CO_2 from the atmosphere or from industrial emissions. These organisms use sunlight to convert CO_2 and water into oxygen and organic matter, a process that helps regulate global carbon levels. Some algae species can capture carbon at a rate several times higher than terrestrial plants, making them a promising tool for climate mitigation.

Algae-based carbon capture systems can be implemented in various ways. Open-pond cultivation systems allow algae to grow in controlled environments using wastewater or seawater, reducing land and freshwater requirements. Alternatively, closed bioreactors enhance efficiency by optimizing light exposure and CO_2 delivery, making them suitable for integration with industrial facilities.

Applications and Benefits

Beyond carbon sequestration, algae-based systems offer multiple environmental and economic benefits. Algae biomass can be converted into biofuels, reducing reliance on fossil fuels while maintaining carbon neutrality. The extracted oils from microalgae can be refined into biodiesel, and residual biomass can be used to produce bioethanol or biogas. These renewable fuels provide a sustainable alternative to conventional energy sources, helping to further reduce emissions.

Additionally, algae-based carbon capture supports sustainable food production. Algae are rich in proteins, vitamins, and omega-3 fatty acids, making them a valuable ingredient for human nutrition and animal feed. The use of algae in agriculture reduces the demand for land-intensive crops, decreasing deforestation and soil degradation.

Algae cultivation also contributes to water purification. Many species absorb excess nutrients such as nitrogen and phosphorus, reducing water pollution and preventing harmful algal blooms. This makes algae-based systems particularly useful in wastewater treatment, where they can capture carbon while improving water quality.

Challenges and Future Prospects

Despite their potential, algae-based carbon capture systems face challenges related to scalability, infrastructure costs, and energy requirements. Large-scale cultivation requires optimal conditions for growth, including sufficient sunlight, nutrients, and controlled CO_2 levels. Additionally, efficient harvesting and processing methods must be developed to ensure economic viability.

Ongoing research focuses on improving algal strain selection, genetic engineering for enhanced CO_2 absorption, and cost-effective harvesting techniques. Governments and industries are exploring policy incentives and financial support mechanisms to integrate algae-based carbon capture into climate strategies.

By combining carbon sequestration with resource recovery, algae-based solutions offer a multifunctional approach to emissions reduction. As technology advances and investment increases, algae-based carbon capture has the potential to become a key component of sustainable climate mitigation efforts.

Bioengineered Crops and Their Impact

Bioengineered crops, also known as genetically modified (GM) or genetically edited crops, are developed through biotechnology to enhance their environmental resilience, productivity, and sustainability. These crops are designed to improve carbon sequestration, reduce greenhouse gas emissions, and minimize reliance on chemical inputs such as synthetic fertilizers and pesticides. By optimizing plant traits, bioengineered crops contribute to emissions reduction and sustainable land management while supporting food security.

Enhancing Carbon Sequestration

Bioengineered crops can enhance carbon sequestration by increasing root biomass, improving photosynthetic efficiency, and promoting soil organic matter accumulation. Deep-rooted crops, such as modified perennial grains, store more carbon in the soil compared to conventional annual crops. These plants transfer a greater portion of their carbon intake into the soil, where it remains stored for extended periods, reducing atmospheric CO_2 levels.

Improved photosynthetic efficiency in bioengineered crops also contributes to greater carbon uptake. Scientists are developing crops with modified photosynthesis pathways, such as enhanced C4 photosynthesis in rice and wheat, to increase carbon fixation rates. These advancements allow plants to grow more efficiently while capturing more carbon per unit of land, making agriculture a more effective carbon sink.

Reducing Greenhouse Gas Emissions

Agriculture is a significant source of CH_4 and N_2O emissions, mainly due to livestock production and fertilizer use. Bioengineered crops help mitigate these emissions by reducing the need for chemical fertilizers and improving nitrogen-use efficiency. For example, nitrogen-fixing crops, such as bioengineered wheat and rice, require fewer nitrogen-based fertilizers, which are a primary source of N_2O emissions.

Additionally, genetically modified crops resistant to pests and diseases reduce the reliance on chemical pesticides. This minimizes the emissions associated with pesticide production and application while lowering environmental contamination. Herbicide-tolerant crops also enable conservation tillage practices, which help retain soil carbon and reduce fuel consumption from mechanized tillage operations.

Improving Drought and Climate Resilience

Climate change increases the frequency of droughts, extreme temperatures, and unpredictable weather patterns. Bioengineered crops designed for drought tolerance require less water and maintain productivity under harsh conditions. These crops help farmers adapt to changing climates while conserving water resources and reducing irrigation-related emissions.

Salt-tolerant bioengineered crops also expand agricultural potential in degraded or salinized soils, reducing the need for land conversion and deforestation. By enabling agriculture in marginal lands, these crops prevent expansion into carbon-rich ecosystems such as forests and wetlands, further contributing to emissions reduction.

Challenges and Future Potential

Despite their benefits, bioengineered crops face regulatory, ethical, and public acceptance challenges. Concerns over genetic modification, biodiversity impacts, and long-term ecosystem effects require careful oversight and transparent research. Ensuring responsible deployment of bioengineered crops involves regulatory approvals, biosafety assessments, and sustainable agricultural practices.

Future advancements in gene-editing technologies, such as CRISPR, offer promising opportunities to develop climate-smart crops with precise modifications. As research progresses and policies support sustainable innovation, bioengineered crops have the potential to play a significant role in reducing agricultural emissions while improving global food security and environmental sustainability.

Bioplastics and Biodegradable Alternatives

Bioplastics and biodegradable alternatives are emerging as sustainable solutions to reduce plastic pollution and lower carbon emissions. Unlike conventional plastics derived from fossil fuels, bioplastics are made from renewable biological sources such as corn starch, sugarcane, algae, and cellulose. These materials offer an environmentally friendly alternative to traditional plastics by reducing reliance on non-renewable resources and improving end-of-life disposal options.

Types of Bioplastics

Bioplastics are categorized based on their origin and degradability. Some are bio-based but not biodegradable, while others are both bio-based and biodegradable. Common types include:

- **Polylactic Acid (PLA)**: Derived from fermented plant sugars, PLA is widely used in packaging, disposable utensils, and textiles. It is compostable under industrial conditions but requires specific environments for complete degradation.
- **Polyhydroxyalkanoates (PHA)**: Produced by bacteria fermenting organic materials, PHAs are fully biodegradable and used in medical applications, packaging, and agricultural films.

- **Bio-based Polyethylene (Bio-PE)**: Made from plant-derived ethanol, Bio-PE functions like conventional polyethylene but is sourced from renewable materials, reducing its carbon footprint.

Environmental Benefits

Bioplastics and biodegradable alternatives contribute to emissions reduction by lowering dependence on petroleum-based plastics. Their production emits fewer greenhouse gases, especially when sourced from sustainably managed biomass. Additionally, biodegradable plastics decompose naturally, reducing plastic waste accumulation in landfills and marine ecosystems.

Another advantage is their role in a circular economy, where bio-based materials return to the environment without causing long-term pollution. When properly composted, biodegradable plastics enrich soil quality and reduce the demand for chemical fertilizers.

Challenges and Considerations

Despite their benefits, bioplastics face challenges related to scalability, cost, and disposal infrastructure. Many biodegradable plastics require industrial composting facilities, which are not widely available. If disposed of in conventional landfills, some bioplastics may not degrade efficiently.

Moreover, large-scale production of bio-based plastics raises concerns about land use competition with food crops. Sustainable sourcing and advances in feedstocks—such as algae and agricultural waste—are crucial to minimizing negative environmental impacts.

Future Outlook

Research is advancing toward next-generation bioplastics with improved degradation rates and lower resource demands. Innovations such as biodegradable coatings, enzyme-assisted decomposition, and bio-based polymers from waste materials hold promise for reducing plastic pollution while maintaining functionality. As governments implement stricter plastic regulations and industries invest in sustainable materials, bioplastics and biodegradable alternatives are expected to play an increasingly vital role in a low-carbon future.

Chapter 3: Financing Bio-Based Solutions

The successful implementation and scaling of bio-based solutions depend not only on technological advancements but also on access to adequate financing. Investment in bio-based initiatives supports emissions reduction, ecosystem restoration, and sustainable land management, helping to transition economies toward more resilient and low-carbon systems. However, financing these solutions requires overcoming challenges related to upfront costs, long-term returns, and policy alignment.

This chapter explores the financial mechanisms that enable the development and deployment of bio-based solutions, including green bonds, carbon markets, impact investing, and public-private partnerships. It examines how funding structures can incentivize businesses, landowners, and governments to adopt sustainable practices while ensuring economic viability. Additionally, the chapter discusses barriers to financing, such as regulatory uncertainties and scalability issues, and highlights potential strategies to attract investment in bio-based initiatives. Understanding the financial landscape is essential for unlocking the full potential of bio-based solutions and integrating them into mainstream sustainability strategies.

Investment trends in bio-based solutions

Investment in bio-based solutions has grown significantly in recent years as governments, businesses, and financial institutions recognize their potential to mitigate climate change, restore ecosystems, and promote sustainable land management. Funding for bio-based initiatives is increasingly seen as a critical component of global sustainability efforts, with investors focusing on innovations that enhance carbon sequestration, replace fossil-based materials, and improve resource efficiency.

Rising Interest in Bio-Based Investments

The global shift toward sustainable finance has led to increased funding for bio-based technologies and projects. Venture capital firms, institutional investors, and impact funds are allocating resources to companies developing bio-based materials, biofuels, and carbon sequestration solutions. Governments are also supporting bio-based industries through subsidies, research grants, and policy incentives that encourage private-sector investment.

Green finance instruments, such as green bonds and sustainability-linked loans, are playing a key role in directing capital toward bio-based initiatives. These financial mechanisms provide funding for projects related to regenerative agriculture, reforestation, and bioplastics, helping businesses transition to low-carbon operations.

Key Sectors Attracting Investment

Several sectors within the bio-based economy are experiencing increased investment:

- **Bio-based Materials**: Companies producing bioplastics, bio-based textiles, and biodegradable packaging are securing funding as industries seek alternatives to petroleum-based products.
- **Bioenergy and Biofuels**: Investments in bioethanol, biodiesel, and next-generation biofuels are expanding as governments implement policies to reduce reliance on fossil fuels.
- **Carbon Sequestration Technologies**: Innovations such as biochar, algae-based carbon capture, and enhanced soil carbon storage are attracting funding from both private and public sources.
- **Sustainable Agriculture and Forestry**: Regenerative farming, agroforestry, and sustainable land-use projects are benefiting from impact investments that prioritize environmental and social benefits.

Challenges in Scaling Investment

Despite growing interest, financing bio-based solutions faces challenges. High upfront costs, long return periods, and regulatory uncertainties can deter investors. Additionally, limited infrastructure for bio-based production and processing can slow market development. Addressing these barriers requires clearer policy frameworks, financial risk mitigation strategies, and stronger collaboration between the public and private sectors.

Future Outlook

As carbon markets expand and sustainability reporting requirements increase, investment in bio-based solutions is expected to grow further. Advancements in biotechnology, combined with supportive financial mechanisms, will drive innovation and scalability. By integrating bio-based investments into mainstream sustainability strategies, financial markets can accelerate the transition toward a more resilient and low-carbon economy.

Green bonds and carbon markets

Green bonds and carbon markets play a crucial role in financing bio-based solutions by providing capital for sustainable projects and creating economic incentives for emissions reduction. These financial instruments help bridge the gap between environmental goals and economic viability, allowing businesses, governments, and investors to support bio-based initiatives that contribute to climate mitigation, ecosystem restoration, and sustainable land management.

Green Bonds: Financing Sustainable Projects

Green bonds are fixed-income financial instruments specifically designed to fund environmentally friendly projects. These bonds provide capital for initiatives such as afforestation, sustainable agriculture, bio-based material production, and bioenergy development. Issued by governments, corporations, and financial institutions, green bonds have gained popularity as investors increasingly seek opportunities aligned with environmental, social, and governance (ESG) criteria.

Key Benefits of Green Bonds for Bio-Based Solutions:

4. **Lower Cost of Capital**: Green bonds often come with favorable interest rates, making them an attractive financing option for large-scale bio-based projects.
5. **Long-Term Investment Potential**: Investors seeking sustainable returns are drawn to bio-based initiatives that generate environmental and economic benefits over time.
6. **Government and Policy Support**: Many governments offer incentives for green bond issuance, helping to scale investment in bio-based industries.

Green bond frameworks, such as those established by the International Capital Market Association (ICMA) and Climate Bonds Initiative (CBI), ensure that funds are allocated to projects with measurable environmental impacts. This transparency helps attract institutional investors, further expanding the pool of available capital for bio-based solutions.

Carbon Markets: Monetizing Emissions Reductions

Carbon markets create financial incentives for reducing greenhouse gas emissions by allowing companies and organizations to buy and sell carbon credits. These markets operate under two main frameworks: compliance markets and voluntary markets.

- **Compliance Carbon Markets**: Regulated by governments or international agreements, these markets require companies to limit emissions and purchase carbon offsets if they exceed their limits. The EU Emissions Trading System (ETS) and California's Cap-and-Trade Program are examples of compliance markets.
- **Voluntary Carbon Markets**: Businesses and individuals participate voluntarily to offset their carbon footprint,

supporting bio-based projects such as reforestation, soil carbon sequestration, and biochar production.

How Bio-Based Solutions Benefit from Carbon Markets:

- **Revenue Generation**: Bio-based projects that sequester carbon or reduce emissions can generate carbon credits, creating a new income stream for landowners and businesses.
- **Encouraging Sustainable Practices**: Carbon pricing encourages industries to invest in bio-based solutions to lower their emissions and reduce offset costs.
- **Market Growth**: With increasing corporate commitments to carbon neutrality, voluntary carbon markets are expanding, driving more investment into bio-based initiatives.

Challenges and Future Opportunities

Despite their potential, green bonds and carbon markets face challenges such as price volatility, regulatory inconsistencies, and concerns over carbon credit integrity. Strengthening market standards, improving carbon accounting methodologies, and enhancing transparency will be critical to ensuring these financial instruments effectively support bio-based solutions.

As climate policies evolve and investor interest in sustainable finance grows, green bonds and carbon markets will continue to drive investment in bio-based initiatives. By integrating these financial mechanisms, bio-based solutions can scale more effectively, accelerating progress toward a low-carbon and resilient global economy.

Role of public-private partnerships

Public-private partnerships (PPPs) play a crucial role in scaling bio-based solutions by combining government support with private sector innovation and investment. These collaborations help bridge financial gaps, facilitate technology transfer, and create enabling environments for sustainable projects. By leveraging the strengths of both sectors, PPPs accelerate the development and deployment of bio-based solutions for emissions reduction, ecosystem restoration, and sustainable land management.

Why Public-Private Partnerships Matter

The transition to a bio-based economy requires significant investment, infrastructure, and policy support. Governments provide regulatory frameworks, incentives, and public funding, while private entities contribute expertise, technology, and capital. This synergy helps overcome financial and operational barriers that may otherwise hinder the adoption of bio-based solutions.

PPPs are particularly valuable in emerging sectors where initial risks and costs are high. They enable pilot projects, de-risk private investments, and establish market confidence for broader adoption. For bio-based industries, these partnerships ensure long-term financial viability while aligning sustainability goals with economic growth.

Key Areas Where PPPs Support Bio-Based Solutions

1. Research and Development (R&D) Initiatives

Governments and private companies collaborate on R&D programs to develop advanced bio-based materials, biofuels, and carbon sequestration technologies. Public funding supports early-stage research, while private sector participation accelerates commercialization. Examples include joint research centers, technology incubators, and government grants that encourage innovation.

2. Infrastructure Development

Scaling bio-based solutions requires specialized infrastructure, such as biorefineries, biochar production facilities, and algae-based carbon capture systems. Public sector investment in infrastructure—through subsidies, tax incentives, and direct funding—encourages private sector involvement. This shared investment model reduces financial risks and accelerates deployment.

3. Carbon Markets and Incentive Programs

Governments establish carbon pricing mechanisms, emissions trading systems, and subsidy programs that incentivize private sector participation in bio-based initiatives. PPPs facilitate the development of standardized carbon credit methodologies for biochar, reforestation, and soil carbon sequestration, making these solutions more financially viable.

4. Capacity Building and Knowledge Transfer

Public institutions provide technical training, education programs, and policy guidance to support bio-based industries. Private companies benefit from access to skilled labor, research collaborations, and policy alignment. This exchange of knowledge ensures that innovations reach market readiness while maintaining environmental integrity.

5. Risk Mitigation and Financial Support

Governments can de-risk private investment in bio-based solutions by offering loan guarantees, blended finance models, and insurance mechanisms. These financial instruments encourage private investors to fund projects that might otherwise be considered too uncertain or capital-intensive.

Challenges and Future Opportunities

Despite their benefits, PPPs face challenges such as regulatory delays, differing risk perceptions, and the need for long-term policy commitments. Ensuring transparency, clear governance structures, and measurable sustainability outcomes is essential for successful partnerships.

As climate policies evolve and demand for bio-based solutions increases, PPPs will play an even greater role in financing and implementing large-scale sustainability projects. Strengthening collaboration between public institutions and private enterprises will be key to accelerating innovation, reducing emissions, and building a resilient bio-based economy.

Incentives for landowners and businesses

To encourage the adoption of bio-based solutions, governments and financial institutions offer various incentives to landowners and businesses. These incentives help offset the costs of transitioning to sustainable practices while making bio-based projects financially viable. By aligning economic benefits with environmental goals, incentive programs drive emissions reduction, ecosystem restoration, and sustainable land management.

Types of Incentives for Landowners

1. Carbon Credit Programs

Landowners who implement bio-based solutions—such as afforestation, regenerative agriculture, or biochar application—can generate carbon credits. These credits can be sold in compliance or voluntary carbon markets, providing an additional revenue stream while supporting climate mitigation.

2. Direct Subsidies and Grants

Governments offer subsidies and grants to encourage sustainable land-use practices. These financial incentives support the adoption of bio-based fertilizers, agroforestry systems, and soil carbon sequestration techniques. Grants often cover a portion of the initial investment, making sustainability-focused projects more accessible to landowners.

3. Tax Incentives and Deductions

Tax incentives reduce financial burdens for landowners who invest in bio-based solutions. Examples include property tax reductions for land conservation, tax credits for carbon sequestration activities, and deductions for adopting sustainable farming practices. These mechanisms encourage long-term environmental stewardship.

4. Payments for Ecosystem Services (PES)

Many governments and private organizations compensate landowners for maintaining and restoring ecosystems that provide environmental benefits. PES programs reward activities such as reforestation, wetland restoration, and soil regeneration, ensuring that conservation efforts are economically sustainable.

Types of Incentives for Businesses

1. Green Bonds and Low-Interest Loans

Businesses investing in bio-based solutions can access green bonds and sustainability-linked loans. These financial instruments offer lower interest rates and favorable repayment terms for projects related to bio-based materials, biofuels, and sustainable land-use practices.

2. R&D Funding

Governments and international organizations provide R&D grants to businesses developing innovative bio-based technologies. Funding supports advancements in bioplastics, bioenergy, and microbial soil enhancements, enabling companies to scale solutions with reduced financial risk.

3. Regulatory Incentives and Fast-Track Approvals

Businesses adopting bio-based solutions may benefit from regulatory incentives, such as streamlined permitting processes or preferential treatment in government procurement contracts. These incentives reduce bureaucratic barriers, accelerating market entry for sustainable innovations.

4. Corporate Sustainability Certifications and Market Benefits

Businesses that integrate bio-based solutions into their supply chains can obtain sustainability certifications, such as organic, fair trade, or carbon-neutral labels. These certifications enhance brand value, attract environmentally conscious consumers, and provide access to premium markets.

Challenges and Future Considerations

Despite the availability of incentives, adoption barriers include complex application processes, inconsistent policy support, and challenges in quantifying environmental benefits. Strengthening incentive frameworks, ensuring policy stability, and improving access to financing will be key to expanding bio-based solutions.

By aligning financial incentives with sustainability objectives, policymakers and industry leaders can accelerate the transition toward bio-based economies. Continued investment in incentive programs will help landowners and businesses implement bio-based solutions at scale, driving long-term environmental and economic benefits.

Barriers to financing and solutions

Financing bio-based solutions presents several challenges that hinder large-scale adoption and implementation. Despite growing interest in sustainable investments, financial constraints, regulatory uncertainties, and market limitations often slow progress. Addressing these barriers requires coordinated efforts from policymakers, financial institutions, and private-sector stakeholders to create a supportive investment environment.

Key Barriers to Financing Bio-Based Solutions

1. High Upfront Costs and Long Payback Periods

Bio-based solutions, such as biochar production, regenerative agriculture, and bio-based materials, require significant initial investments in infrastructure, technology, and training. Many investors are hesitant to commit capital due to long payback periods and uncertainties regarding return on investment.

Solution: Governments and financial institutions can provide low-interest loans, grants, and tax incentives to reduce financial risks for businesses and landowners. Blended finance models, combining public and private funding, can also help lower costs and encourage long-term investment.

2. Limited Access to Capital for Small-Scale Projects

Many bio-based initiatives are developed at a local or regional scale, making it difficult for small businesses, farmers, and landowners to secure funding. Traditional financial institutions often favor large-scale, high-return projects, leaving smaller initiatives underfunded.

Solution: Microfinance programs, green bonds, and crowdfunding platforms can provide accessible funding for small and medium-sized enterprises (SMEs) and community-led projects. Expanding impact investment funds focused on sustainable agriculture and land restoration can also bridge financing gaps.

3. Regulatory Uncertainty and Policy Inconsistencies

Unclear or inconsistent policies regarding carbon pricing, land use, and renewable energy incentives create financial uncertainty for investors. Without stable regulations, bio-based projects face difficulties in planning and securing long-term funding.

Solution: Governments should establish clear, long-term policy frameworks that support bio-based investments. Strengthening carbon pricing mechanisms, standardizing sustainability certifications, and ensuring regulatory stability can attract investors and facilitate project development.

4. Difficulty in Measuring Environmental and Financial Returns

Investors often struggle to quantify the long-term environmental and economic benefits of bio-based solutions. Unlike traditional investments, bio-based initiatives require robust monitoring systems to track carbon sequestration, biodiversity improvements, and financial performance.

Solution: Advancing digital tools, such as satellite monitoring, blockchain-based carbon tracking, and AI-driven impact assessments, can improve data transparency and investment confidence. Establishing standardized metrics for measuring environmental returns can also help investors make informed decisions.

Chapter 4: Governance and Policy Frameworks for Bio-Based Solutions

Effective governance and policy frameworks are essential for scaling bio-based solutions and integrating them into national and global sustainability strategies. Clear regulations, financial incentives, and institutional support help create a stable investment environment while ensuring that bio-based initiatives contribute meaningfully to emissions reduction, ecosystem restoration, and sustainable land management.

This chapter examines the role of governance in shaping bio-based policies, from international agreements and carbon pricing mechanisms to national regulations and certification standards. It explores how governments, regulatory bodies, and industry stakeholders collaborate to develop policies that promote bio-based solutions while addressing challenges such as regulatory uncertainty, market integration, and compliance enforcement. Additionally, the chapter discusses the importance of harmonizing policies across sectors to create a cohesive framework that supports long-term adoption and innovation.

By understanding the governance structures that guide bio-based solutions, policymakers and industry leaders can enhance their effectiveness, ensuring they contribute to climate resilience and sustainable economic growth.

Overview of governance in bio-based solutions

Governance plays a crucial role in the development, regulation, and implementation of bio-based solutions. Effective governance frameworks ensure that bio-based initiatives align with climate goals, contribute to emissions reduction, and promote sustainable land management. These frameworks include policies, regulations, market mechanisms, and institutional support that facilitate the adoption and scaling of bio-based technologies.

Key Governance Aspects in Bio-Based Solutions

1. Regulatory Frameworks and Policy Support

Governments establish policies that define how bio-based solutions can be implemented, monitored, and incentivized. These regulations cover areas such as land use, carbon sequestration, sustainable agriculture, and industrial applications of bio-based materials. Policy instruments, including subsidies, tax credits, and grants, encourage businesses and landowners to adopt bio-based practices.

International agreements, such as the Paris Agreement, also shape national governance strategies by setting emissions reduction targets and promoting nature-based solutions. Countries integrate bio-based strategies into their climate policies to meet sustainability commitments while supporting economic growth.

2. Carbon Pricing and Market Mechanisms

Governance structures influence how bio-based solutions participate in carbon markets and emissions trading schemes. Carbon pricing mechanisms, such as carbon taxes and cap-and-trade systems, create financial incentives for businesses and landowners to invest in carbon sequestration and sustainable practices.

For example, biochar production, regenerative agriculture, and afforestation projects can generate carbon credits that are traded in compliance or voluntary carbon markets. Transparent and well-regulated market mechanisms ensure the credibility of these credits, preventing issues such as double counting or overestimation of emissions reductions.

3. Certification and Standardization

To build trust in bio-based solutions, governance frameworks include certification programs and sustainability standards. These standards define criteria for bio-based products, ensuring they meet environmental, social, and economic benchmarks. Certifications such as organic, fair trade, and carbon-neutral labels enhance market acceptance and encourage responsible production practices.

4. Institutional Collaboration and Multi-Stakeholder Engagement

Governance of bio-based solutions requires collaboration between governments, businesses, research institutions, and civil society organizations. PPPs play a key role in financing and scaling bio-based projects, while knowledge-sharing platforms support innovation and best practices.

National and international policy frameworks

National and international policy frameworks play a vital role in advancing bio-based solutions by setting regulatory guidelines, financial incentives, and sustainability targets. These frameworks help integrate bio-based initiatives into climate action strategies, ensuring their alignment with emissions reduction, ecosystem restoration, and sustainable land management goals. Effective policies create a stable investment environment while encouraging innovation and large-scale adoption of bio-based technologies.

International Policy Frameworks

1. The Paris Agreement and Climate Commitments

The Paris Agreement, adopted under the United Nations Framework Convention on Climate Change (UNFCCC), sets global targets for emissions reduction, with bio-based solutions playing a key role in achieving these goals. Countries submit Nationally Determined Contributions (NDCs), outlining their climate strategies, including the use of bio-based carbon sequestration techniques, sustainable agriculture, and bioenergy.

2. The European Green Deal

The European Green Deal aims to make Europe climate-neutral by 2050, emphasizing bio-based solutions in its sustainability strategies. The EU's Bioeconomy Strategy promotes bio-based industries, sustainable land use, and circular economy principles. The Common Agricultural Policy (CAP) supports farmers adopting regenerative practices and bio-based technologies through subsidies and funding programs.

3. UN Sustainable Development Goals (SDGs)

Several SDGs, including Goal 13 (Climate Action), Goal 15 (Life on Land), and Goal 12 (Responsible Consumption and Production), align with bio-based solutions. International organizations promote bio-based initiatives by integrating them into sustainable development projects, ensuring their role in global environmental governance.

4. Carbon Pricing and International Market Mechanisms

The Carbon Offsetting and Reduction Scheme for International Aviation (CORSIA) under the International Civil Aviation Organization (ICAO) allows airlines to offset emissions using bio-based carbon sequestration projects. Additionally, Article 6 of the Paris Agreement facilitates international carbon trading, enabling countries to finance bio-based projects through global carbon markets.

National Policy Frameworks

1. Renewable Energy and Bioeconomy Policies

Many countries incorporate bio-based solutions into their national energy policies by promoting biofuels, biogas, and bioenergy. Government incentives support the development of bio-based industries, reducing reliance on fossil fuels. National bioeconomy strategies in countries such as the United States, Germany, and Brazil focus on scaling bio-based products and technologies.

2. Agricultural and Land-Use Policies

Policies promoting sustainable agriculture, afforestation, and soil carbon sequestration provide financial incentives for farmers and landowners to adopt bio-based solutions. Conservation programs, such as the U.S. Conservation Reserve Program (CRP) and the EU's Agri-Environment Climate Measures (AECM), reward landowners for implementing regenerative practices.

3. Regulatory Standards and Certification

Governments establish regulatory frameworks to ensure bio-based solutions meet sustainability and safety standards. Certification programs for bioplastics, biofuels, and organic farming enhance transparency and market confidence, ensuring responsible adoption of bio-based solutions.

Carbon pricing and emissions trading integration

Carbon pricing and ETS provide financial incentives for emissions reduction by placing a cost on greenhouse gas (GHG) emissions. These mechanisms encourage industries to adopt sustainable practices, invest in carbon sequestration, and integrate bio-based solutions into their operations. By creating economic value for emissions reductions, carbon pricing and trading markets drive investment in bio-based technologies, sustainable agriculture, and ecosystem restoration.

Carbon Pricing Mechanisms

Carbon pricing is implemented through two primary approaches: carbon taxes and cap-and-trade systems (ETS).

1. Carbon Taxes

A carbon tax directly sets a price per ton of CO_2 emitted, encouraging businesses to reduce their carbon footprint. Countries such as Sweden, Canada, and Japan have introduced carbon taxes to incentivize low-carbon alternatives. Bio-based solutions benefit from carbon taxes as industries seek cost-effective ways to lower emissions, including the use of biochar for soil carbon sequestration, biofuels for energy production, and algae-based carbon capture technologies.

2. Cap-and-Trade ETS

Under cap-and-trade systems, governments set an overall emissions limit, distributing or auctioning emissions allowances to regulated industries. Companies that emit less than their allowances can sell excess credits, while those exceeding limits must purchase additional allowances or invest in emissions reduction projects.

The EU Emissions Trading System (EU ETS) is the largest carbon market, covering power generation, manufacturing, and aviation. Other markets, such as California's Cap-and-Trade Program and China's National ETS, provide additional models for integrating carbon pricing into economic activities.

Integration of Bio-Based Solutions in Emissions Trading

Bio-based solutions can generate tradable carbon credits through carbon sequestration, emissions reductions, and sustainable land management. Key areas where bio-based projects participate in carbon markets include:

1. Carbon Sequestration Projects

- Reforestation and afforestation projects generate carbon credits by capturing CO_2 through tree planting.

- Soil carbon sequestration, including no-till farming, agroforestry, and biochar application, qualifies for carbon credit programs.
- Blue carbon ecosystems (mangroves, seagrasses) contribute to high-value carbon credits due to their long-term sequestration potential.

2. Bioenergy and Low-Carbon Alternatives

7. Biofuels and biogas projects reduce reliance on fossil fuels, earning credits for emissions displacement.
8. Biodegradable materials and bioplastics replace carbon-intensive plastics, contributing to overall emissions reduction.

Challenges and Future Considerations

Despite its potential, integrating bio-based solutions into carbon markets faces challenges such as:

- Verification and monitoring difficulties, requiring standardized methodologies for carbon accounting.
- Market volatility and price fluctuations, affecting investment certainty.
- Regulatory inconsistencies between jurisdictions, creating compliance uncertainties.

Future advancements in remote sensing, AI-based monitoring, and policy harmonization will enhance the credibility of bio-based carbon credits, increasing their role in emissions trading. Strengthening carbon pricing frameworks will drive greater investment in bio-based solutions, accelerating their adoption as part of global climate strategies.

Regulatory challenges and opportunities

Effective regulation is essential for scaling bio-based solutions, ensuring they contribute to emissions reduction, ecosystem restoration, and sustainable land management. However, regulatory challenges—including inconsistent policies, market barriers, and compliance complexities—often hinder large-scale adoption. At the same time, well-designed regulations create opportunities by establishing clear standards, financial incentives, and market confidence. Addressing regulatory gaps is critical to maximizing the potential of bio-based solutions.

Key Regulatory Challenges

1. Policy Inconsistencies and Fragmentation

Bio-based solutions operate across multiple sectors, including agriculture, energy, and industry. However, regulatory frameworks often lack coordination, creating uncertainty for businesses and investors. Differences in national policies, certification standards, and carbon accounting methods complicate market integration and investment decisions.

Solution: Governments should align bio-based regulations with broader climate policies, ensuring consistency in carbon pricing mechanisms, emissions reduction targets, and sustainability standards. International cooperation can facilitate harmonized regulations that support cross-border investments.

2. Lack of Standardized Carbon Accounting for Bio-Based Solutions

Carbon sequestration projects, such as biochar application, soil carbon storage, and reforestation, require accurate measurement and verification to participate in carbon markets. However, variations in methodologies for quantifying carbon sequestration make it difficult for bio-based projects to secure carbon credits.

Solution: Developing standardized measurement frameworks and certification processes can improve the credibility of bio-based carbon offsets. Advances in remote sensing, blockchain-based carbon tracking, and AI-driven monitoring can enhance transparency and reliability.

3. Market Access Barriers

Many bio-based products, including bioplastics, biofuels, and biodegradable materials, face regulatory hurdles related to approval processes, labeling requirements, and trade restrictions. Lengthy regulatory approvals delay market entry, reducing the competitiveness of bio-based alternatives compared to fossil-based products.

Solution: Streamlining regulatory approval processes, expanding government procurement of bio-based products, and enforcing clear labeling standards can support market growth. Policies that phase out fossil-based alternatives in favor of bio-based solutions can accelerate adoption.

Regulatory Opportunities for Scaling Bio-Based Solutions

1. Incentive Programs and Subsidies

Governments can introduce financial incentives, such as tax credits, grants, and subsidies, to encourage investment in bio-based solutions. Programs supporting regenerative agriculture, bio-based materials, and carbon sequestration create economic advantages for businesses adopting sustainable practices.

2. Strengthening Compliance Mechanisms

Clear enforcement of sustainability regulations—such as carbon pricing mandates, emissions caps, and land-use policies—ensures that bio-based solutions receive long-term regulatory support. Strong compliance mechanisms create a level playing field, attracting investment in climate-friendly technologies.

3. Expanding International Cooperation

Collaboration between governments, industry groups, and research institutions can facilitate knowledge sharing and policy alignment. Global agreements on bio-based product certification, emissions reduction targets, and sustainable trade practices can enhance regulatory stability.

Standardization and certification of bio-based products

Standardization and certification play a crucial role in ensuring the credibility, safety, and market acceptance of bio-based products. Clear standards help define sustainability criteria, regulate product performance, and create consumer trust. Certification programs verify compliance with environmental and ethical benchmarks, making it easier for businesses and policymakers to integrate bio-based solutions into mainstream markets.

Importance of Standardization

Standardization establishes consistent definitions, measurement methods, and quality criteria for bio-based products. Without clear standards, inconsistencies in labeling, carbon accounting, and biodegradability claims can create confusion and hinder market growth. Well-defined regulations ensure that bio-based solutions meet sustainability objectives while maintaining performance and durability.

For example, bio-based materials such as bioplastics and biofuels require standardized testing to confirm their composition, biodegradability, and environmental impact. Similarly, biochar used for soil enhancement must meet purity and stability standards to ensure its effectiveness in carbon sequestration.

Key Certification Programs for Bio-Based Products

1. Bio-Based Content Certification

- **USDA Certified BioPreferred (United States)**: Labels products based on their percentage of bio-based content.
- European Bio-Based Certification Scheme (EU): Ensures compliance with EU sustainability directives for bio-based materials.

2. Sustainability and Environmental Impact Certification

- **Forest Stewardship Council (FSC)**: Certifies sustainable forestry practices for bio-based products such as wood and paper.
- **Roundtable on Sustainable Biomaterials (RSB)**: Establishes sustainability criteria for biofuels and bio-based materials, ensuring ethical sourcing and lifecycle sustainability.

3. Biodegradability and Compostability Standards

- **EN 13432 (EU) & ASTM D6400 (US)**: Certify industrial compostability for bioplastics and packaging materials.
- **OK Compost & TÜV Austria**: Verify biodegradability under specific environmental conditions.

Challenges and Future Considerations

Despite the benefits of standardization and certification, challenges remain. Some bio-based products require complex lifecycle assessments to determine their environmental impact. Certification costs can be a barrier for small producers, limiting market entry. Additionally, differences in global standards can create trade barriers, making it difficult for bio-based products to gain international recognition.

Harmonizing global standards, expanding third-party certification programs, and improving consumer awareness will strengthen the credibility of bio-based solutions. As demand for sustainable products increases, standardization and certification will be critical in ensuring that bio-based alternatives effectively contribute to climate goals, circular economy principles, and sustainable development.

Chapter 5: Land Management Strategies for Bio-Based Approaches

Sustainable land management is essential for maximizing the benefits of bio-based solutions in emissions reduction, ecosystem restoration, and resource efficiency. By integrating bio-based approaches into land use planning, agriculture, and forestry, it is possible to enhance carbon sequestration, improve soil health, and promote biodiversity while maintaining economic productivity.

This chapter explores key land management strategies that support bio-based solutions, including sustainable agriculture, agroforestry, restorative grazing, and the conservation of carbon-rich ecosystems such as wetlands and peatlands. It examines how these approaches contribute to long-term soil stability, water retention, and carbon storage. Additionally, the chapter highlights the challenges of balancing conservation with land-use demands and the need for policies that incentivize sustainable land management.

By implementing science-based and nature-driven land management strategies, governments, businesses, and landowners can create resilient landscapes that contribute to climate mitigation while ensuring food security and environmental sustainability.

Sustainable agriculture and agroforestry

Sustainable agriculture and agroforestry play a vital role in bio-based solutions by enhancing carbon sequestration, improving soil health, and promoting biodiversity while maintaining food production. These land management practices integrate ecological principles to reduce greenhouse gas emissions, improve water efficiency, and build resilient farming systems. By combining sustainable farming techniques with tree-based systems, agroforestry further strengthens environmental and economic benefits.

Sustainable Agriculture for Climate Mitigation

Sustainable agriculture minimizes the environmental impact of food production while maintaining or increasing yields. Key practices include:

1. Conservation Tillage and No-Till Farming

Conservation tillage reduces soil disturbance, preventing carbon loss and enhancing soil organic matter. No-till farming improves soil structure, increases water retention, and promotes microbial activity, leading to greater carbon sequestration.

2. Cover Cropping and Crop Rotation

Cover crops, such as legumes and grasses, protect soil from erosion, improve nutrient cycling, and enhance carbon storage. Crop rotation diversifies plant species, reducing soil depletion and the need for chemical fertilizers while supporting long-term agricultural sustainability.

3. Organic and Regenerative Farming

Regenerative agricultural practices, including composting, natural pest management, and minimal synthetic input use, restore soil health and increase carbon capture. By promoting diverse plant cover and reducing synthetic fertilizers, regenerative agriculture enhances microbial activity and improves resilience to climate change.

4. Water-Efficient Farming Practices

Sustainable irrigation methods, such as drip irrigation and rainwater harvesting, reduce water waste while maintaining crop productivity. Improved water management prevents soil degradation, conserves natural resources, and enhances ecosystem resilience.

Agroforestry as a Bio-Based Solution

Agroforestry integrates trees, shrubs, and perennial plants into agricultural systems, creating multifunctional landscapes that support climate mitigation and adaptation.

1. Carbon Sequestration through Tree Integration

Trees and perennial plants in agroforestry systems absorb atmospheric CO_2, storing carbon in biomass and soils. Compared to conventional agriculture, agroforestry sequesters more carbon while improving land productivity.

2. Soil Enrichment and Erosion Control

Tree roots stabilize soils, preventing erosion and nutrient loss. Leaf litter from trees enriches soil organic matter, enhancing fertility and moisture retention. Agroforestry systems reduce dependency on synthetic fertilizers by naturally recycling nutrients.

3. Biodiversity Enhancement

Agroforestry supports diverse plant and animal species by creating varied habitats. Pollinators, beneficial insects, and wildlife thrive in these systems, contributing to ecological balance and improved crop yields.

4. Economic and Livelihood Benefits

Farmers benefit from diversified income streams through tree-based products, including fruits, nuts, timber, and medicinal plants. Agroforestry increases climate resilience by reducing vulnerability to extreme weather events.

Restorative Grazing and Soil Carbon Enhancement

Restorative grazing and soil carbon enhancement are key land management strategies that contribute to emissions reduction, soil regeneration, and ecosystem resilience. By optimizing livestock grazing patterns and implementing soil improvement techniques, these approaches support carbon sequestration, biodiversity restoration, and sustainable agricultural productivity.

Restorative Grazing for Carbon Sequestration

Restorative grazing, also known as rotational or holistic grazing, involves managing livestock movements to mimic natural grazing patterns. This approach prevents overgrazing, promotes plant regrowth, and enhances soil carbon storage. Key benefits include:

1. Improved Grassland Carbon Sequestration

Grasslands naturally absorb CO_2 through photosynthesis, storing carbon in plant biomass and soils. Properly managed grazing allows for continuous grass regrowth, increasing carbon capture and preventing soil degradation. Well-maintained pastures can act as long-term carbon sinks.

2. Enhanced Soil Organic Matter

Livestock grazing stimulates root growth and organic matter deposition in soils. The natural breakdown of plant residues and manure contributes to soil carbon pools, improving fertility and water retention. This process strengthens soil structure, reducing erosion and nutrient loss.

3. Biodiversity and Ecosystem Resilience

Restorative grazing supports diverse plant communities by preventing the dominance of a single species. By rotating livestock across pastures, different plant species thrive, improving habitat quality for pollinators, insects, and soil microorganisms. Enhanced biodiversity increases ecosystem stability and resilience to climate change.

4. Reduction in Methane Emissions

While livestock production contributes to CH_4 emissions, improved grazing practices can offset these emissions by increasing soil carbon storage. Integrating forage species that enhance digestive efficiency—such as legumes and high-fiber grasses—reduces methane output from ruminant digestion.

Soil Carbon Enhancement Strategies

Beyond grazing management, additional soil improvement techniques further increase carbon sequestration and soil health:

1. Compost and Organic Amendments

Applying compost, biochar, and organic residues enriches soil organic matter, stabilizing carbon while enhancing microbial activity. These materials improve soil aeration, nutrient availability, and moisture retention.

2. Cover Crops and Perennial Grasses

Integrating cover crops in grazing systems adds organic matter to soils, improving carbon retention. Perennial grasses, with deep root systems, increase soil carbon storage while enhancing drought resistance and erosion control.

3. No-Till and Reduced Soil Disturbance

Minimizing soil disturbance through no-till farming and reduced tillage prevents the release of stored carbon. These practices maintain soil integrity, allowing natural carbon sequestration to continue without disruption.

Wetlands, peatlands, and carbon-rich ecosystems

Wetlands, peatlands, and other carbon-rich ecosystems are among the most effective natural carbon sinks, playing a crucial role in climate mitigation and biodiversity conservation. These ecosystems store vast amounts of carbon, regulate water cycles, and provide critical habitats for wildlife. However, they face increasing threats from land conversion, agriculture, and climate change, leading to carbon release and ecosystem degradation. Protecting and restoring these landscapes is essential for reducing greenhouse gas emissions and ensuring long-term environmental resilience.

The Role of Wetlands in Carbon Sequestration

Wetlands, including marshes, swamps, and mangroves, capture and store carbon by accumulating organic material in water-saturated soils. These anaerobic conditions slow decomposition, preventing the release of CO_2 and CH_4. Key benefits of wetlands include:

1. Carbon Storage and Climate Regulation

Wetlands absorb CO_2 through photosynthesis, locking carbon into plant biomass and soil. Unlike terrestrial ecosystems, wetlands store carbon for centuries with minimal risk of release, provided they remain undisturbed.

2. Flood Control and Water Filtration

Wetlands act as natural buffers, reducing flood risks by absorbing excess water. They also filter pollutants, improving water quality and supporting freshwater biodiversity.

3. Coastal Resilience and Blue Carbon Ecosystems

Mangroves, seagrasses, and salt marshes—often referred to as blue carbon ecosystems—are highly efficient carbon sinks. These coastal wetlands store carbon at higher rates than forests and provide protection against storm surges, erosion, and sea-level rise.

Peatlands as Global Carbon Reservoirs

Peatlands, including bogs and fens, cover only 3% of the Earth's land surface but store nearly 25% of global soil carbon. This makes them one of the most important ecosystems for carbon sequestration. Peat forms through the accumulation of partially decomposed plant material in waterlogged, oxygen-poor conditions, preventing carbon release.

1. Preventing Carbon Loss from Degraded Peatlands

Draining peatlands for agriculture, forestry, and development leads to rapid oxidation of stored carbon, releasing CO_2 into the atmosphere. Peatland degradation accounts for a significant portion of global land-use emissions. Restoring degraded peatlands through rewetting and conservation prevents further emissions and enhances ecosystem functions.

2. Biodiversity and Hydrological Stability

Peatlands provide unique habitats for rare and specialized plant and animal species. They also regulate groundwater levels, reducing drought risks and maintaining hydrological stability.

The Need for Conservation and Restoration

Despite their importance, wetlands and peatlands continue to be lost at alarming rates. Effective conservation strategies include legal protection, sustainable land management practices, and incentive programs for ecosystem restoration. Rewetting peatlands, restoring mangrove forests, and implementing wetland conservation policies can enhance carbon sequestration while improving biodiversity and water security.

Urban and peri-urban land management integration

Integrating bio-based solutions into urban and peri-urban land management is essential for enhancing climate resilience, reducing emissions, and improving environmental quality. As cities expand, sustainable land-use strategies must balance development with ecosystem conservation, ensuring that natural processes continue to provide essential services such as carbon sequestration, air purification, and water regulation. By incorporating bio-based approaches into urban planning, municipalities can create greener, more livable spaces that contribute to long-term sustainability.

The Role of Bio-Based Solutions in Urban Areas

1. Green Infrastructure and Nature-Based Solutions

Urban green infrastructure—such as parks, green roofs, urban forests, and wetlands—enhances carbon sequestration while mitigating the urban heat island effect. Trees and vegetation absorb CO_2, filter pollutants, and regulate local temperatures, improving air quality and reducing energy demands for cooling.

Green corridors and connected green spaces also support biodiversity, providing habitat for pollinators, birds, and other species in urban environments. Expanding tree canopies and urban forests increases carbon storage while enhancing recreational spaces and public health benefits.

2. Sustainable Water Management

Bio-based approaches play a key role in urban water management by improving stormwater retention and reducing flood risks. Permeable pavements, constructed wetlands, and rain gardens help capture and filter runoff, preventing water pollution and increasing groundwater recharge. These systems integrate natural hydrological processes, reducing pressure on traditional drainage infrastructure.

Additionally, wastewater treatment facilities can incorporate bio-based technologies such as algae-based filtration and microbial bioremediation to improve water quality while capturing carbon. These solutions contribute to circular water economies, where water resources are recycled and reused efficiently.

3. Urban Agriculture and Peri-Urban Food Systems

Integrating sustainable agriculture into urban and peri-urban areas enhances food security while promoting bio-based carbon sequestration. Community gardens, vertical farming, and agroforestry systems reduce reliance on external food supply chains, lowering transportation emissions and increasing local resilience.

Peri-urban landscapes provide opportunities for regenerative farming practices that restore soil health, enhance biodiversity, and capture carbon. Urban composting programs further support circular economies by converting organic waste into nutrient-rich soil amendments, reducing landfill emissions and improving agricultural productivity.

Challenges and Opportunities

Despite their benefits, integrating bio-based solutions into urban planning faces challenges such as land-use conflicts, policy fragmentation, and financial constraints. High land costs and competing development priorities can limit the expansion of green infrastructure and sustainable land management practices.

Opportunities exist through policy incentives, public-private partnerships, and regulatory frameworks that encourage green building standards and sustainable urban design. Cities that prioritize bio-based solutions in zoning laws, climate adaptation plans, and investment strategies can drive long-term environmental and economic benefits.

Challenges and conflicts in land use

Balancing economic development, environmental conservation, and social needs in land use planning presents significant challenges and conflicts. As demand for agricultural expansion, urbanization, and infrastructure grows, competition for land increases, often leading to deforestation, habitat loss, and reduced carbon sequestration potential. Addressing these conflicts requires integrated policies that support sustainable land management while considering economic and social priorities.

Key Challenges in Land Use Management

1. Competing Demands for Land

Land is a finite resource, and different sectors compete for its use. Agriculture, forestry, urban expansion, and industrial activities often overlap, leading to conflicts over resource allocation. For example, expanding agricultural lands to meet food demand can result in deforestation, reducing carbon sinks and biodiversity. Similarly, rapid urban growth encroaches on natural areas, increasing environmental degradation.

2. Deforestation and Land Degradation

Large-scale deforestation for agriculture, logging, and infrastructure development releases stored carbon into the atmosphere, contributing to climate change. Land degradation due to unsustainable farming practices, overgrazing, and soil erosion further reduces the land's ability to sequester carbon and support biodiversity.

3. Conflicts Between Conservation and Development

Efforts to conserve forests, wetlands, and other carbon-rich ecosystems sometimes face opposition from industries seeking to use the land for economic activities. Protected areas may restrict local communities' access to land, creating tensions between conservation goals and economic livelihoods.

4. Land Tenure and Governance Issues

Unclear land ownership rights and weak governance structures can hinder sustainable land management. In some regions, lack of formal land tenure prevents communities from investing in long-term conservation practices. Additionally, conflicting policies between national and local governments can create regulatory uncertainty, slowing the implementation of bio-based solutions.

Strategies for Conflict Resolution

1. Integrated Land-Use Planning

Holistic land-use planning ensures that agricultural, industrial, and conservation needs are balanced. Policies that promote mixed-use landscapes, such as agroforestry and sustainable urban planning, help mitigate land-use conflicts.

2. Incentives for Sustainable Practices

Financial incentives, such as payments for ecosystem services (PES) and carbon credit programs, encourage landowners to adopt sustainable land-use practices while maintaining economic viability.

3. Strengthening Land Tenure and Governance

Clarifying land rights and enforcing transparent governance structures empower communities to engage in sustainable land management while reducing conflicts over resource use.

Chapter 6: Bio-Based Innovations in Sustainable Industry

The transition to a sustainable economy requires industries to adopt bio-based innovations that reduce reliance on fossil fuels, minimize waste, and lower greenhouse gas emissions. Bio-based materials, bioenergy, and bioprocessing technologies offer scalable solutions that align with circular economy principles while promoting environmental and economic resilience.

This chapter explores key bio-based innovations transforming industries, including biodegradable materials, biorefineries, biofuels, and enzyme-based manufacturing. It examines how these technologies contribute to emissions reduction, resource efficiency, and waste management. Additionally, the chapter highlights the challenges of scaling bio-based industries, such as production costs, infrastructure requirements, and regulatory considerations.

By integrating bio-based solutions into industrial practices, businesses can enhance sustainability, reduce environmental impacts, and contribute to a low-carbon future. Strengthening research, investment, and policy support will be essential for accelerating the adoption of bio-based innovations across sectors.

Bio-based materials in construction, textiles, packaging

Bio-based materials are transforming industries by providing sustainable alternatives to fossil fuel-based products. In construction, textiles, and packaging, these materials reduce carbon emissions, enhance resource efficiency, and contribute to a circular economy. By replacing traditional materials with bio-based alternatives, industries can lower environmental impacts while promoting innovation in sustainable manufacturing.

Bio-Based Materials in Construction

The construction sector is a significant contributor to global emissions due to the high carbon footprint of concrete, steel, and synthetic insulation materials. Bio-based alternatives offer sustainable solutions that reduce embodied carbon while improving energy efficiency.

1. Engineered Wood and Bamboo

- Cross-laminated timber (CLT) and laminated veneer lumber (LVL) are strong, lightweight alternatives to concrete and steel. These materials sequester carbon while offering high structural integrity.
- Bamboo is a rapidly renewable resource with high strength, making it a viable option for flooring, paneling, and structural elements.

2. Bio-Based Insulation

9. Hempcrete (a mixture of hemp fibers, lime, and water) provides natural insulation, reduces carbon emissions, and improves indoor air quality.
10. Mycelium-based insulation, derived from fungal networks, is biodegradable, fire-resistant, and offers effective thermal performance.

3. Algae-Based Concrete Alternatives

Algae-derived materials, such as biogenic limestone cement, capture carbon during production, reducing emissions associated with traditional cement manufacturing.

Bio-Based Materials in Textiles

The textile industry is one of the largest sources of environmental pollution due to synthetic fibers and chemical-intensive production. Bio-based textiles provide a sustainable alternative, reducing dependency on fossil fuels while improving biodegradability.

1. Plant-Based Fibers

- Hemp, flax (linen), and organic cotton require fewer resources compared to conventional cotton and synthetic fibers. These materials biodegrade naturally and have a lower environmental footprint.
- Bamboo fabric is a sustainable alternative to rayon and polyester, offering breathability and antibacterial properties.

2. Mycelium and Algae-Based Textiles

- Mycelium leather is an eco-friendly substitute for animal leather, requiring fewer resources and producing less waste.
- Algae-derived fabrics provide biodegradable alternatives for synthetic textiles, reducing microplastic pollution.

Bio-Based Materials in Packaging

Packaging waste is a major contributor to environmental pollution, particularly single-use plastics. Bio-based alternatives offer sustainable solutions that reduce plastic dependency and improve biodegradability.

1. Bioplastics and Compostable Packaging

- PLA, derived from cornstarch or sugarcane, provides a biodegradable alternative to petroleum-based plastics.
- PHA are compostable biopolymers produced by bacteria, offering a sustainable alternative to traditional plastic packaging.

2. Mycelium and Seaweed-Based Packaging

- Mycelium packaging is a biodegradable alternative to Styrofoam, made from fungal growth on agricultural waste.

- Seaweed-based films replace plastic wraps, offering an edible and compostable solution for food packaging.

Biorefineries and Sustainable Chemical Production

Biorefineries play a crucial role in the transition to a sustainable economy by converting biomass into bio-based fuels, chemicals, and materials. Unlike conventional refineries, which rely on fossil fuels, biorefineries use renewable biological resources, such as agricultural waste, algae, and forestry residues, to produce energy and chemicals with a lower environmental footprint. This approach supports emissions reduction, resource efficiency, and circular economy principles.

The Role of Biorefineries in Sustainable Industry

Biorefineries integrate various processing technologies to extract valuable compounds from biomass. These facilities produce biofuels, bioplastics, biochemicals, and bio-based textiles, replacing petroleum-based products and reducing carbon emissions. The biorefinery model is similar to petroleum refining but focuses on renewable feedstocks to minimize waste and maximize material recovery.

1. Biofuels and Renewable Energy Production

- **Ethanol and Biodiesel**: First-generation biofuels, such as ethanol from corn and sugarcane and biodiesel from vegetable oils, reduce reliance on fossil fuels and lower greenhouse gas emissions.
- **Advanced Biofuels**: Second- and third-generation biofuels, including cellulosic ethanol from agricultural residues and algae-based biofuels, offer higher efficiency and fewer land-use conflicts.
- **Biogas and Biohydrogen**: Anaerobic digestion of organic waste produces biogas, a renewable energy source, while

69

gasification processes generate biohydrogen for clean energy applications.

2. Bio-Based Chemicals and Sustainable Industrial Products

- **Platform Chemicals**: Biorefineries produce platform chemicals, such as lactic acid, succinic acid, and furfural, which serve as building blocks for bio-based plastics, solvents, and coatings.
- **Green Solvents and Surfactants**: Derived from plant-based sources, these chemicals replace petroleum-derived solvents in industrial applications, reducing toxicity and environmental impact.
- **Biopolymers and Bioplastics**: PLA and PHA are biodegradable plastics produced in biorefineries, offering alternatives to fossil-based plastics.

3. Circular Economy and Waste Valorization

- **Agricultural and Forestry Residue Utilization**: Biorefineries use crop residues, wood chips, and food waste as feedstocks, reducing landfill waste and promoting resource efficiency.
- **Co-Product Recovery**: Biorefineries generate valuable byproducts, such as biochar for soil improvement, lignin for biochemicals, and protein-rich biomass for animal feed.
- **Carbon Capture Integration**: Some biorefineries incorporate carbon capture technologies to further reduce emissions, creating carbon-negative industrial processes.

Challenges and Future Prospects

Despite their potential, biorefineries face challenges such as high capital costs, infrastructure limitations, and competition with established fossil-based industries. Scaling bio-based chemical production requires technological advancements, supportive policies, and financial incentives.

Investment in research and development, policy frameworks for sustainable sourcing, and market incentives for bio-based products will drive the growth of biorefineries. As industries transition to renewable alternatives, biorefineries will play an essential role in reducing emissions, promoting circularity, and advancing sustainable chemical production.

Biofuels and Their Role in Decarbonization

Biofuels play a critical role in the transition to a low-carbon economy by providing renewable alternatives to fossil fuels. Produced from biological feedstocks such as crops, algae, and organic waste, biofuels help reduce GHG emissions in the transportation, industrial, and energy sectors. Their ability to integrate into existing fuel infrastructure makes them a viable option for decarbonization while supporting energy security and economic sustainability.

Types of Biofuels

Biofuels are categorized based on their feedstocks and production methods:

1. First-Generation Biofuels

- **Bioethanol**: Produced through the fermentation of sugar- and starch-rich crops like corn, sugarcane, and wheat, bioethanol is blended with gasoline to reduce carbon emissions. Common blends include E10 (10% ethanol) and E85 (85% ethanol).
- **Biodiesel**: Derived from vegetable oils, animal fats, or used cooking oil, biodiesel can replace petroleum-based diesel in transportation and industrial applications. It is often blended with conventional diesel in varying proportions (e.g., B20, B100).

2. Second-Generation Biofuels

- **Cellulosic Ethanol**: Made from non-food biomass, including agricultural residues, forestry waste, and dedicated energy crops, cellulosic ethanol offers higher carbon savings and avoids competition with food production.
- **Hydrotreated Vegetable Oil (HVO)**: A refined form of biodiesel, HVO has improved combustion properties and can be used in aviation and heavy-duty transport.

3. Third-Generation Biofuels

- **Algae-Based Biofuels**: Algae can produce high yields of bio-oil, which can be refined into biodiesel, bioethanol, and even biojet fuel. These fuels offer significant carbon reduction potential with minimal land use.
- **Biohydrogen**: Produced from biomass gasification or microbial fermentation, biohydrogen is a promising renewable fuel for fuel cells and clean energy applications.

The Role of Biofuels in Decarbonization

1. Emissions Reduction in Transportation

The transportation sector is a major contributor to global CO_2 emissions. Biofuels reduce lifecycle emissions by absorbing CO_2 during feedstock growth, offsetting emissions released during combustion. Advanced biofuels, such as cellulosic ethanol and algae-based fuels, achieve even greater carbon savings compared to first-generation options.

2. Sustainable Aviation and Shipping Fuels

Biofuels play a key role in decarbonizing aviation and maritime industries, where electrification remains challenging. Sustainable aviation fuels (SAFs) derived from biomass or waste oils can reduce airline emissions by up to 80%. Similarly, bio-based marine fuels offer a lower-emission alternative for shipping.

3. Integration with Existing Infrastructure

Unlike some renewable energy sources, biofuels can be blended with conventional fuels and used in existing engines, pipelines, and refineries. This reduces transition costs and allows for gradual adoption without requiring new infrastructure.

Challenges and Future Outlook

Despite their benefits, biofuels face challenges related to land use, production costs, and scalability. Expanding sustainable feedstock sources, improving conversion technologies, and implementing strong sustainability policies will be essential for maximizing biofuels' role in decarbonization.

Enzymatic and Microbial Processing for the Circular Bioeconomy

Enzymatic and microbial processing are key technologies driving the circular bioeconomy by enabling the efficient conversion of organic waste, biomass, and renewable feedstocks into valuable bio-based products. These biological processes replace traditional chemical methods, reducing energy consumption, emissions, and reliance on fossil-based resources. By leveraging the capabilities of enzymes and microbes, industries can improve waste valorization, enhance resource efficiency, and contribute to sustainable production systems.

The Role of Enzymatic Processing in Bio-Based Industries

Enzymes are biological catalysts that accelerate chemical reactions, making them essential in various industrial applications. Their specificity and efficiency allow for targeted breakdown and synthesis of organic materials, supporting the production of biofuels, bioplastics, and green chemicals.

1. Enzymatic Biomass Conversion for Biofuels

- **Cellulases and Hemicellulases**: These enzymes break down plant cellulose and hemicellulose into fermentable sugars, which are then converted into bioethanol. This process is crucial for producing second-generation biofuels from agricultural residues and woody biomass.
- **Lipases and Proteases**: Used in biodiesel production, these enzymes facilitate the transesterification of oils and fats into biofuels, reducing the need for harsh chemical catalysts.

2. Enzymatic Plastic Degradation and Recycling

- **PET-Degrading Enzymes**: Enzymes such as PETase and MHETase can break down polyethylene terephthalate (PET) plastics into their monomer components, enabling efficient recycling and reuse.
- **Biodegradable Polymer Production**: Enzymatic synthesis of PHA and PLA supports the development of compostable and bio-based plastics.

3. Enzymatic Waste Treatment and Upcycling

- **Waste-to-Protein Conversion**: Enzymes facilitate the breakdown of food waste and agricultural residues into protein-rich animal feed, reducing food system losses.
- **Lignin Valorization**: Lignin-degrading enzymes enable the conversion of lignin-rich waste from the paper and biofuel industries into high-value chemicals, such as vanillin and bio-based adhesives.

Microbial Processing for Circular Biomanufacturing

Microbes, including bacteria, fungi, and yeast, play a crucial role in the bioeconomy by transforming organic materials into bio-based chemicals, fuels, and materials.

1. Microbial Fermentation for Sustainable Biochemicals

- **Lactic Acid Bacteria**: Used in fermentation to produce biodegradable plastics (PLA) and bio-based solvents.
- **Yeast and Bacteria for Biorefineries**: Engineered microbes convert sugars into ethanol, butanol, and bio-based polymers, supporting fossil-free production pathways.

2. Bioremediation and Waste Decomposition

- **Microbial Digestion of Organic Waste**: Anaerobic digestion by microbes produces biogas, which can be used as a renewable energy source.
- **Heavy Metal and Pollutant Breakdown**: Microorganisms help detoxify contaminated soils and wastewater, enabling ecosystem restoration.

Scaling Bio-Based Innovations for Mainstream Industries

Bio-based innovations have the potential to transform industries by reducing emissions, enhancing resource efficiency, and supporting the transition to a circular economy. However, scaling these solutions for mainstream adoption requires overcoming economic, technological, and policy challenges. Widespread integration of bio-based materials, fuels, and processes into industrial operations depends on investment, infrastructure development, and regulatory support.

Key Challenges in Scaling Bio-Based Innovations

1. High Production Costs and Market Competition

Many bio-based products, such as bioplastics, biofuels, and bio-based chemicals, face high production costs compared to fossil-based alternatives. Advanced bio-manufacturing processes often require specialized infrastructure and supply chains, making large-scale production financially challenging.

Solution: Government incentives, subsidies, and economies of scale can help reduce costs. Increased investment in R&D will improve production efficiency and cost competitiveness.

2. Infrastructure and Supply Chain Limitations

Scaling bio-based solutions requires infrastructure for biomass processing, bio-refining, and distribution. Many existing industrial systems are designed for fossil-based products, creating barriers to large-scale integration of bio-based alternatives.

Solution: Developing biorefinery networks, improving logistics for biomass collection, and retrofitting existing production facilities can facilitate the transition.

3. Regulatory Uncertainty and Standardization

Inconsistent regulations across regions create uncertainty for businesses investing in bio-based innovations. Lack of standardized sustainability certifications can also limit market confidence in bio-based products.

Solution: Governments can establish clear policies, create sustainability standards, and implement carbon pricing mechanisms to support bio-based industries.

4. Consumer Awareness and Market Demand

Consumer adoption of bio-based products is essential for scaling their impact. However, limited awareness and higher costs may slow market uptake.

Solution: Public awareness campaigns, corporate sustainability commitments, and eco-labeling programs can drive consumer demand and encourage businesses to transition to bio-based alternatives.

Opportunities for Large-Scale Adoption

- **Public-Private Partnerships**: Collaboration between governments, industry leaders, and research institutions can accelerate commercialization and investment in bio-based solutions.
- **Circular Economy Integration**: Bio-based innovations align with circular economy principles by reducing waste, repurposing materials, and lowering environmental impact.
- **Advancements in Biotechnology**: Innovations in synthetic biology, enzyme engineering, and microbial processing continue to enhance bio-based production efficiency and scalability.

Chapter 7: Measuring the Impact of Bio-Based Solutions

The effectiveness of bio-based solutions in reducing emissions, restoring ecosystems, and promoting sustainable land management must be assessed through reliable measurement frameworks. Accurate impact measurement ensures that bio-based initiatives deliver meaningful environmental benefits while supporting policy development, investment decisions, and industry adoption.

This chapter explores key methodologies for evaluating the impact of bio-based solutions, including lifecycle assessments (LCA), carbon accounting, and biodiversity monitoring. It examines how data-driven approaches help quantify emissions reductions, resource efficiency, and ecosystem improvements. Additionally, the chapter discusses challenges in standardizing measurement frameworks and the role of emerging technologies such as remote sensing, AI, and blockchain in improving transparency and accountability.

By implementing robust impact measurement strategies, governments, businesses, and researchers can optimize bio-based solutions, strengthen sustainability policies, and enhance public confidence in bio-based innovations.

Tools and Frameworks for Impact Assessment

Measuring the impact of bio-based solutions requires standardized tools and frameworks to evaluate their effectiveness in reducing emissions, enhancing resource efficiency, and restoring ecosystems. Accurate assessments ensure that bio-based initiatives contribute meaningfully to sustainability goals while supporting decision-making for policymakers, investors, and businesses.

Life Cycle Assessment (LCA)

LCA is a widely used methodology for evaluating the environmental impact of products, processes, or systems across their entire lifecycle. It measures key indicators such as carbon footprint, energy consumption, and resource use from raw material extraction to disposal.

Applications:

- Comparing bio-based materials with fossil-based alternatives in terms of emissions and energy efficiency.
- Assessing the sustainability of biofuels by considering feedstock cultivation, processing, transportation, and combustion.
- Evaluating the environmental benefits of biochar, bioplastics, and sustainable agriculture practices.

Carbon Accounting and Carbon Footprint Analysis

Carbon accounting frameworks quantify GHG emissions reductions achieved through bio-based solutions. These methodologies follow internationally recognized standards such as:

11. **The Greenhouse Gas Protocol**: Provides a structured approach for measuring direct and indirect emissions from business operations.
12. **ISO 14067**: Specifies requirements for calculating the carbon footprint of products.
13. **IPCC Guidelines for National Greenhouse Gas Inventories**: Used by governments to track emissions reductions from land-use changes, reforestation, and bio-based energy systems.

Applications:

- Measuring carbon sequestration from biochar, reforestation, and soil carbon storage.

- Calculating emissions reductions from bio-based energy transitions.
- Supporting participation in carbon markets and emissions trading schemes.

Biodiversity and Ecosystem Impact Monitoring

Assessing the ecological impact of bio-based solutions involves tracking changes in biodiversity, soil health, and ecosystem resilience. Key frameworks include:

- **The IUCN Red List and Biodiversity Indicators**: Used to monitor the effects of bio-based land management practices on species conservation.
- **The Soil Health Card System**: Evaluates improvements in soil fertility, organic matter, and microbial activity due to bio-based agricultural practices.
- **The Natural Capital Protocol**: Helps businesses integrate ecosystem services valuation into decision-making.

Applications:

- Monitoring the impact of agroforestry and regenerative agriculture on biodiversity.
- Assessing habitat restoration benefits from wetland and peatland conservation projects.
- Evaluating the role of bio-based urban infrastructure in enhancing green spaces.

Remote Sensing and Digital Tools

Advancements in technology have improved impact measurement through satellite imagery, AI-driven analytics, and blockchain-based tracking systems. These tools enhance transparency and real-time monitoring of bio-based initiatives.

Applications:

- Using satellite data to track deforestation, land-use changes, and carbon sequestration.
- Employing AI models to analyze soil carbon levels and crop health.
- Implementing blockchain for verifiable carbon credit transactions.

Remote Sensing, AI, and Digital Monitoring

Advancements in remote sensing, artificial intelligence (AI), and digital monitoring are transforming the way bio-based solutions are assessed, tracked, and optimized. These technologies provide real-time data on emissions reduction, carbon sequestration, and ecosystem health, enabling better decision-making for governments, businesses, and environmental organizations. By improving measurement accuracy and scalability, digital tools enhance the credibility and effectiveness of bio-based initiatives.

Remote Sensing for Environmental Monitoring

Remote sensing uses satellite imagery, aerial drones, and ground-based sensors to collect large-scale environmental data. These technologies are crucial for tracking land-use changes, biomass growth, and carbon sequestration.

Applications in Bio-Based Solutions:

- **Carbon Sequestration Tracking**: Satellites measure vegetation density and forest carbon storage using spectral imaging and LIDAR technology. These assessments support reforestation, agroforestry, and soil carbon projects.
- **Land-Use and Deforestation Monitoring**: High-resolution satellite imagery detects land-cover changes, identifying deforestation, wetland degradation, and urban expansion that impact carbon sinks.

- **Agricultural Productivity Analysis**: Remote sensing helps assess crop health, soil moisture, and nutrient levels, optimizing sustainable farming and bio-based agriculture.

Organizations such as NASA, the European Space Agency (ESA), and private satellite firms provide remote sensing data that support impact assessments for bio-based initiatives.

Artificial Intelligence for Data Analysis and Prediction

AI enhances impact measurement by processing vast amounts of environmental data, identifying patterns, and predicting future trends. Machine learning algorithms analyze satellite imagery, sensor data, and climate models to improve the accuracy of sustainability assessments.

Applications in Bio-Based Solutions:

- **Soil Carbon Monitoring**: AI models analyze soil composition, microbial activity, and carbon sequestration potential, enabling precision land management.
- **Biodiversity and Ecosystem Health Assessment**: AI-driven image recognition identifies species diversity, tracking how bio-based land management practices affect wildlife populations.
- **Climate Impact Forecasting**: AI-powered predictive models estimate how bio-based solutions influence emissions reductions, providing insights for policymakers and investors.

AI-driven decision support systems help industries optimize resource use, reduce waste, and implement targeted sustainability strategies.

Digital Monitoring and Blockchain for Transparency

Blockchain and digital monitoring systems improve accountability and traceability in bio-based solutions by securely recording environmental data and transactions. These technologies help verify carbon credits, track supply chains, and ensure compliance with sustainability standards.

Applications in Bio-Based Solutions:

- **Carbon Credit Verification**: Blockchain platforms track carbon sequestration projects, preventing fraud and ensuring transparent emissions reductions.
- **Supply Chain Traceability**: Digital systems verify sustainable sourcing of bio-based materials, such as bioplastics, biofuels, and regenerative agriculture products.
- **Real-Time Environmental Reporting**: IoT sensors and mobile applications collect real-time data on air quality, water usage, and ecosystem restoration, supporting adaptive land management strategies.

Life Cycle Assessments of Bio-Based Products

LCA is a systematic method used to evaluate the environmental impacts of bio-based products throughout their entire life cycle. From raw material extraction to production, distribution, use, and disposal, LCA provides a comprehensive analysis of energy use, emissions, and resource consumption. By identifying areas for improvement, LCA helps businesses, policymakers, and researchers develop more sustainable bio-based solutions.

Key Stages of Life Cycle Assessment

LCA follows a structured approach to assess the full environmental footprint of bio-based products. The main stages include:

- Raw Material Extraction and Cultivation

- Bio-based products are derived from renewable sources such as crops, algae, forestry residues, and organic waste.

- Agricultural inputs, including water use, fertilizers, and land use, are assessed for their environmental impact.
- Carbon sequestration during plant growth is factored into overall emissions calculations.

- Manufacturing and Processing

- The transformation of raw materials into bio-based fuels, plastics, textiles, or chemicals requires energy and chemical inputs.
- Process emissions, waste generation, and efficiency improvements are evaluated to determine the overall sustainability of production.

- Distribution and Transportation

- LCA considers the energy used and emissions generated from transporting bio-based products from production sites to consumers.
- Differences between locally sourced and imported bio-based products influence their environmental impact.

- Use Phase and Performance

- The functional benefits of bio-based products are compared to conventional alternatives, such as the durability of bioplastics versus fossil-based plastics.
- Indirect impacts, such as reduced dependency on non-renewable resources, are considered.

- End-of-Life Disposal and Circularity

- LCA assesses whether bio-based products can be composted, recycled, or biodegraded, reducing landfill waste.
- Energy recovery from waste biomass or composting emissions is factored into impact calculations.

Environmental Benefits and Trade-Offs

1. Carbon Footprint Reduction

- Many bio-based products have lower carbon footprints compared to fossil-based alternatives due to carbon sequestration during biomass growth.
- However, emissions from land-use changes or energy-intensive processing may offset some benefits.

1. Water and Land Use Considerations

- LCA identifies potential trade-offs, such as high water consumption in biofuel production or competition between food and bio-based feedstocks.
- Sustainable sourcing strategies help minimize negative land-use impacts.

Ecosystem Service Valuation and Decision-Making

Ecosystem services are the benefits that natural ecosystems provide to society, including carbon sequestration, water purification, soil fertility, and biodiversity support. Valuing these services is essential for integrating environmental considerations into economic and policy decision-making. By quantifying the contributions of ecosystems, governments, businesses, and communities can make informed choices that balance conservation, resource use, and sustainable development.

Understanding Ecosystem Service Valuation

Ecosystem service valuation assigns monetary, social, or ecological value to natural processes that benefit human well-being. These services are typically categorized into four main groups:

- **Provisioning Services**: Natural resources such as food, water, timber, and medicinal plants.
- **Regulating Services**: Climate regulation, carbon sequestration, air and water purification, and flood control.

- **Supporting Services**: Soil formation, nutrient cycling, and habitat maintenance for biodiversity.
- **Cultural Services**: Recreation, tourism, aesthetic value, and cultural heritage.

Valuation methods help quantify these benefits, providing a basis for policy incentives, conservation efforts, and sustainable land management strategies.

Methods for Valuing Ecosystem Services

Market-Based Valuation

- Direct market pricing assesses ecosystem services based on their economic value in commercial markets, such as timber pricing or carbon credit trading.
- Payments for ecosystem services (PES) programs compensate landowners for maintaining forests, wetlands, and biodiversity.

Cost-Based Approaches

- Avoided cost analysis estimates the economic value of ecosystem services by measuring the cost of replacing them with artificial alternatives (e.g., natural flood control vs. engineered levees).
- Restoration cost assessments determine the investment needed to rehabilitate degraded ecosystems.

Willingness to Pay and Social Valuation

- Contingent valuation surveys gauge how much individuals or businesses are willing to pay for ecosystem conservation or restoration.
- Travel cost methods estimate the economic value of cultural services by assessing tourism and recreational spending.

Role of Ecosystem Service Valuation in Decision-Making

Policy and Land-Use Planning

Governments use valuation data to design conservation policies, set land-use priorities, and allocate resources efficiently.

Integration of ecosystem service values into environmental impact assessments helps mitigate ecological degradation.

Corporate Sustainability Strategies

- Businesses incorporate ecosystem service valuation in supply chain decisions, carbon offset programs, and sustainability reporting.
- Investments in nature-based solutions, such as reforestation and wetland restoration, contribute to long-term corporate resilience.

Climate and Conservation Finance

- Financial institutions use valuation frameworks to guide investments in conservation projects and bio-based innovations.
- Carbon markets and biodiversity credits provide financial incentives for maintaining ecosystem services.

Addressing Uncertainties and Improving Methodologies

Accurately measuring the impact of bio-based solutions requires reliable data, standardized methodologies, and robust assessment frameworks. However, uncertainties in carbon accounting, ecosystem service valuation, and life cycle assessments (LCA) can affect decision-making and investment confidence. Addressing these uncertainties is essential for ensuring the credibility and effectiveness of bio-based initiatives.

Key Sources of Uncertainty

Variability in Environmental Conditions

- Differences in climate, soil quality, and land-use practices impact the performance of bio-based solutions, making it difficult to apply generalized impact estimates.
- Seasonal changes and extreme weather events influence carbon sequestration rates and ecosystem restoration outcomes.

Data Gaps and Measurement Challenges

- Limited availability of long-term field data on carbon storage, biodiversity benefits, and soil health creates gaps in impact assessments.
- Remote sensing and AI-based monitoring tools are improving data collection but still require calibration and validation.

Inconsistent Methodologies

- Different carbon accounting frameworks use varying assumptions for baseline emissions, sequestration rates, and leakage effects.
- Lack of standardized methodologies across jurisdictions leads to inconsistencies in reporting and verification.

Strategies for Reducing Uncertainty

Standardization of Measurement Protocols

- Developing globally accepted standards for carbon accounting, LCA, and ecosystem valuation improves comparability and credibility.
- Harmonizing methodologies across regulatory bodies and certification programs enhances transparency.

Advancements in Monitoring Technologies

- Expanding the use of satellite imagery, blockchain-based tracking, and IoT sensors increases accuracy in impact measurement.
- AI-driven data analytics help refine models for predicting emissions reductions and biodiversity gains.

Continuous Research and Adaptive Management

- Ongoing field studies and pilot projects provide updated insights into bio-based solution performance under different conditions.
- Adaptive management approaches allow for flexibility in policy design based on evolving scientific knowledge.

Chapter 8: Overcoming Barriers to Bio-Based Innovation

Despite the growing recognition of bio-based solutions in emissions reduction, ecosystem restoration, and sustainable land management, several barriers hinder their large-scale adoption. Challenges such as high production costs, limited infrastructure, regulatory complexities, and market competition with fossil-based alternatives slow the transition to a bio-based economy. Addressing these obstacles requires coordinated efforts from policymakers, businesses, investors, and researchers to create an enabling environment for innovation and commercialization.

This chapter explores the key barriers to scaling bio-based solutions and examines strategies to overcome them. It discusses the role of financial incentives, policy reforms, technological advancements, and public-private partnerships in accelerating the adoption of bio-based innovations. By identifying practical solutions, this chapter highlights pathways to integrate bio-based approaches into mainstream industries and global sustainability efforts.

Key Adoption Challenges: Cost, Scalability, Infrastructure

The widespread adoption of bio-based solutions faces significant challenges related to cost, scalability, and infrastructure. While bio-based technologies offer sustainable alternatives to fossil-based industries, high production expenses, limited scalability, and inadequate infrastructure slow their integration into mainstream markets. Addressing these barriers is essential to accelerating the transition toward a bio-based economy.

High Production Costs and Market Competition

Expensive Raw Materials and Processing

- Many bio-based products rely on specialized feedstocks, such as algae, lignocellulosic biomass, or agricultural residues, which can be costly to source and process.
- Compared to fossil-based counterparts, bio-based alternatives often require advanced technologies that increase operational costs.

Economies of Scale Challenges

14. Many bio-based industries remain in early stages, operating at lower production volumes, making it difficult to achieve cost reductions through economies of scale.
15. Large-scale production of bio-based materials, fuels, and chemicals requires significant upfront investment before costs can become competitive.

Price Competition with Fossil-Based Products

- Fossil-based industries benefit from established supply chains, government subsidies, and economies of scale, making bio-based alternatives appear less cost-effective.
- Without financial incentives, consumers and businesses may opt for cheaper conventional materials over bio-based options.

Scalability Barriers

Limited Biomass Availability

- Expanding bio-based production requires sustainable biomass sourcing without causing land-use conflicts, deforestation, or food supply competition.
- Over-reliance on certain feedstocks, such as corn for biofuels, can strain resources and lead to unintended environmental trade-offs.

R&D Gaps

- Scaling bio-based solutions requires ongoing investment in R&D to improve efficiency, yield, and performance.
- Emerging technologies, such as bioengineered enzymes and synthetic biology, need further development to lower production costs and increase commercial viability.

Regulatory and Certification Hurdles

- Lack of standardized regulations and certification frameworks creates uncertainty for investors and businesses looking to scale bio-based innovations.
- Complex approval processes for bio-based materials and biofuels slow down market entry.

Infrastructure Limitations

Insufficient Processing and Manufacturing Facilities

- Bio-based industries require specialized biorefineries, fermentation facilities, and processing plants, which are not yet widely available.
- Retrofitting existing fossil-based infrastructure to accommodate bio-based production requires significant capital investment.

Inadequate Distribution and Logistics

- Transporting biomass feedstocks and bio-based products efficiently remains a logistical challenge, especially in regions with underdeveloped supply chains.
- Bio-based fuels require infrastructure modifications, such as updated pipelines, storage facilities, and fueling stations.

Policy and Regulatory Hurdles

The successful adoption of bio-based solutions depends on clear, supportive policy frameworks and regulatory structures. However, inconsistent policies, lengthy approval processes, and unclear sustainability standards create significant challenges for businesses, investors, and researchers seeking to scale bio-based innovations. Overcoming these regulatory hurdles is essential to ensuring the widespread adoption of bio-based solutions across industries.

Inconsistent and Fragmented Regulations

Variability in National and Regional Policies

- Different countries and regions apply varying regulations to bio-based products, creating compliance challenges for global businesses.
- The absence of internationally harmonized standards makes it difficult to develop unified sustainability criteria for bio-based fuels, materials, and chemicals.

Conflicting Policies Across Sectors

- Bio-based solutions span multiple industries, including agriculture, energy, and manufacturing, each governed by distinct regulatory frameworks.
- Misaligned policies can create unintended trade-offs, such as agricultural subsidies favoring food crops over bio-based feedstocks, limiting raw material availability.

Lengthy Approval and Certification Processes

Complex Licensing for Bio-Based Products

- Many bio-based materials, including bioplastics and biofuels, require extensive testing and regulatory approvals before entering the market.
- Certification processes can be slow, costly, and vary between jurisdictions, delaying commercialization.

Challenges in Carbon Credit and Incentive Programs

- Carbon credit schemes for bio-based carbon sequestration, such as soil carbon storage or biochar application, often lack standardized methodologies.
- Businesses seeking to participate in emissions trading markets may struggle to verify carbon reductions due to inconsistencies in carbon accounting rules.

Lack of Clear Sustainability Standards

Defining Sustainability Criteria

- While bio-based solutions aim to reduce environmental impact, not all bio-based products are inherently sustainable.
- Without clear sustainability criteria, some biofuels and bio-based materials risk contributing to land-use change, deforestation, and resource depletion.

Certification and Labeling Gaps

- The absence of universally accepted certification systems for bio-based products can lead to greenwashing and consumer confusion.
- Strengthening eco-labeling programs and third-party verification systems is essential for building market trust in bio-based innovations.

Strategies for Policy Improvement

Harmonizing Regulations and Standards

- Governments and international organizations should work toward standardizing sustainability benchmarks and regulatory approval processes.
- Aligning carbon credit methodologies, eco-labeling, and emissions reporting systems will enhance market confidence in bio-based solutions.

Streamlining Approval Processes

- Reducing bureaucratic delays in licensing and certification can accelerate the commercialization of bio-based technologies.
- Fast-track regulatory pathways for sustainable bio-based products can incentivize businesses to innovate.

Strengthening Financial and Policy Incentives

- Expanding tax incentives, research grants, and public-private partnerships can encourage investment in bio-based solutions.
- Integrating bio-based targets into national climate policies will drive demand and market adoption.

Behavioral and Cultural Resistance

The transition to bio-based solutions faces significant behavioral and cultural resistance, as individuals, businesses, and industries often hesitate to adopt new practices and technologies. This resistance stems from familiarity with conventional systems, perceived risks, cost concerns, and a lack of awareness about the benefits of bio-based alternatives. Overcoming these barriers requires targeted education, incentives, and policy measures to drive widespread acceptance and adoption.

Consumer Resistance to Bio-Based Products

Perceptions of Performance and Reliability

- Many consumers are hesitant to switch to bio-based products due to concerns about quality, durability, or functionality compared to conventional options.
- Skepticism about biodegradable materials, biofuels, and plant-based alternatives can slow market adoption, even

when these products offer comparable or superior performance.

Price Sensitivity and Cost Perception

- Bio-based products often have higher initial costs than fossil-based alternatives due to limited economies of scale and higher production expenses.
- Consumers may prioritize affordability over sustainability, particularly in price-sensitive markets where bio-based alternatives are not yet widely available.

Lack of Awareness and Misinformation

2. Many consumers are unaware of the environmental benefits of bio-based solutions, leading to a preference for conventional products.
3. Greenwashing and misleading sustainability claims contribute to confusion, making it difficult for consumers to distinguish truly sustainable options.

Industry and Business Resistance

Risk Aversion and Reluctance to Change

- Businesses accustomed to traditional materials, supply chains, and production processes may be reluctant to invest in bio-based alternatives.
- Concerns about supply chain reliability, production scalability, and regulatory uncertainty discourage companies from transitioning to new bio-based models.

Infrastructure and Operational Challenges

2. Many industries rely on fossil-based infrastructure that is not easily adaptable to bio-based alternatives.

3. Transitioning to bio-based production requires investments in new equipment, training, and supply chain restructuring, which can be seen as disruptive and costly.

Resistance from Established Industries

- Fossil fuel, petrochemical, and conventional agriculture industries may oppose the growth of bio-based solutions to protect their market dominance.
- Lobbying efforts and policy influence from established sectors can create barriers to regulatory support for bio-based innovations.

Strategies to Overcome Behavioral and Cultural Resistance

Public Awareness and Education Campaigns

- Providing clear, science-based information about the benefits of bio-based solutions can help shift consumer perceptions and build trust.
- Certification programs and eco-labeling initiatives improve transparency, making it easier for consumers to identify sustainable products.

Incentives for Adoption

- Financial incentives, such as tax credits, subsidies, and grants, encourage businesses and consumers to transition to bio-based alternatives.
- Policies that promote green procurement and sustainable supply chains help drive demand for bio-based solutions.

Industry Collaboration and Policy Support

- Public-private partnerships can accelerate research, investment, and large-scale adoption of bio-based innovations.

- Governments can implement regulatory frameworks that gradually phase out fossil-based products, creating a smoother transition for businesses and consumers.

Knowledge Transfer and Capacity-Building

Effective knowledge transfer and capacity-building are essential for scaling bio-based solutions and integrating them into mainstream industries. Sharing expertise, best practices, and technical skills helps bridge the gap between research, policy, and industry implementation. By strengthening education, training, and collaboration, stakeholders can accelerate the adoption of bio-based innovations and enhance their long-term impact.

The Importance of Knowledge Transfer

Bridging Research and Industry

- Advances in bio-based technologies often remain within academic and research institutions, limiting their application in real-world settings.
- Strengthening connections between researchers, businesses, and policymakers ensures that scientific innovations translate into scalable industry solutions.

Overcoming Technical and Practical Barriers

- Many businesses and policymakers lack the technical expertise needed to implement bio-based solutions effectively.
- Knowledge-sharing initiatives, such as workshops and training programs, equip stakeholders with the skills required for adoption and integration.

Enhancing Policy and Decision-Making

- Policymakers require evidence-based insights to develop regulatory frameworks that support bio-based industries.
- Open access to scientific data and real-world case studies improves policy design, ensuring regulations align with sustainability goals.

Strategies for Effective Knowledge Transfer

Education and Training Programs

- Universities and technical institutes play a key role in training professionals in bio-based industries.
- Vocational programs and online courses provide accessible learning opportunities for farmers, entrepreneurs, and industry leaders.

Industry-Academic Partnerships

- Collaborative research projects between universities and businesses drive innovation by combining theoretical knowledge with practical applications.
- Industry-sponsored research initiatives help commercialize bio-based technologies while providing funding for further development.

Knowledge-Sharing Platforms

- Online databases, open-access journals, and digital knowledge hubs facilitate the exchange of best practices and technical information.
- Conferences, forums, and networking events create opportunities for cross-sector collaboration.

Capacity-Building for Sustainable Implementation

Strengthening Local Expertise

- Capacity-building initiatives empower communities, businesses, and policymakers to develop region-specific bio-based solutions.
- Training programs for farmers, landowners, and industry workers promote sustainable practices and long-term resilience.

Public-Private Partnerships

- Governments, businesses, and non-governmental organizations (NGOs) can collaborate to provide funding, mentorship, and technology transfer programs.
- Joint initiatives ensure that bio-based solutions are accessible, scalable, and tailored to different industries and regions.

Policy Support for Knowledge Dissemination

- Governments can invest in knowledge hubs, research grants, and exchange programs to accelerate the spread of bio-based expertise.
- Incentivizing businesses to invest in employee training ensures a skilled workforce for bio-based industries.

Strategies to Accelerate Adoption

The widespread adoption of bio-based solutions requires targeted strategies that address financial, regulatory, technological, and behavioral barriers. Scaling these innovations across industries depends on coordinated efforts from governments, businesses, and research institutions. By implementing supportive policies, financial incentives, and knowledge-sharing initiatives, stakeholders can accelerate the transition to a bio-based economy.

Financial and Market-Based Incentives

Subsidies and Tax Benefits

- Governments can offer subsidies and tax credits to reduce the production costs of bio-based materials, biofuels, and sustainable agriculture practices.
- Financial incentives encourage businesses to invest in bio-based innovations and transition away from fossil-based alternatives.

Carbon Pricing and Emissions Trading

- Expanding carbon pricing mechanisms and emissions trading systems (ETS) can provide financial rewards for companies implementing bio-based solutions.
- Businesses that invest in carbon sequestration through biochar, agroforestry, or soil carbon storage can generate revenue from carbon credits.

Public and Private Investment in Infrastructure

- Governments and investors can fund the development of biorefineries, processing facilities, and supply chain infrastructure to support large-scale production.
- Expanding green financing options, such as sustainability-linked loans, can help companies transition to bio-based models.

Policy and Regulatory Support

Standardization and Certification

- Establishing clear sustainability standards for bio-based products ensures market credibility and consumer trust.
- Regulatory frameworks should harmonize certification programs across industries and regions.

Green Public Procurement

- Governments can set procurement policies that prioritize bio-based products in infrastructure, construction, and packaging.
- Public sector demand for bio-based alternatives can drive large-scale market adoption.

Technology and Knowledge Sharing

R&D Investment

- Expanding funding for bio-based research helps develop cost-effective and scalable technologies.
- Collaboration between universities, startups, and industries accelerates innovation.

Education and Workforce Training

- Training programs equip workers with the skills needed to support bio-based industries.
- Public awareness campaigns promote consumer acceptance and demand for bio-based products.

Chapter 9: Future Prospects for Bio-Based Climate Action

Bio-based solutions are emerging as key components of global climate action, offering pathways to reduce emissions, enhance carbon sequestration, and promote sustainable resource management. As advancements in biotechnology, materials science, and digital monitoring improve the efficiency and scalability of bio-based innovations, their role in addressing climate challenges is expected to expand significantly.

This chapter explores the future trajectory of bio-based solutions, examining the potential for technological breakthroughs, evolving policy frameworks, and market expansion. It also considers the challenges that remain, including scalability, economic viability, and regulatory alignment. By understanding these opportunities and barriers, stakeholders can better position bio-based solutions as integral components of a low-carbon, resilient economy.

Emerging Trends in Biotechnology and Synthetic Biology

Biotechnology and synthetic biology are driving the next generation of bio-based solutions for climate action, offering innovative ways to reduce emissions, enhance carbon sequestration, and create sustainable materials. Advances in genetic engineering, metabolic pathway optimization, and biofabrication are improving the efficiency, scalability, and economic viability of bio-based alternatives to fossil-derived products. These emerging trends have the potential to transform multiple industries, including energy, agriculture, and manufacturing, by enabling more sustainable production processes.

Advances in Bioengineering for Carbon Sequestration

Genetically Engineered Crops for Carbon Capture

- Scientists are developing plants with enhanced photosynthesis and deeper root systems to increase carbon sequestration in soil.
- Bioengineered crops can absorb more atmospheric CO_2 while improving soil organic matter and nutrient retention.

Synthetic Biology for Algae-Based Carbon Capture

16. Researchers are optimizing algae strains to absorb CO_2 more efficiently and convert it into biofuels or biopolymers.
17. Algae-based carbon capture systems are being integrated into industrial facilities to reduce emissions in manufacturing and power generation.

Bio-Based Materials and Circular Economy Innovations

Microbial Production of Bioplastics

- Synthetic biology is enabling microbes, such as bacteria and yeast, to produce biodegradable polymers like PHA and PLA.
- These bioplastics offer sustainable alternatives to petroleum-based plastics, reducing plastic waste and microplastic pollution.

Mycelium-Based Biomaterials

- Fungi-based materials are being used to create sustainable packaging, insulation, and leather alternatives.
- Mycelium-derived products require minimal inputs, decompose naturally, and offer a low-carbon alternative to synthetic materials.

Sustainable Biofuels and Biochemicals

Advanced Biofuels from Engineered Microorganisms

- Synthetic biology is improving the efficiency of microbial fermentation for bioethanol, biodiesel, and biohydrogen production.
- Engineered microbes can break down non-food biomass, reducing competition with food supplies and improving sustainability.

Biochemicals for Industrial Applications

- Scientists are engineering microorganisms to produce bio-based chemicals, such as bio-derived solvents, adhesives, and coatings.
- These biochemicals replace fossil-based inputs in manufacturing, reducing emissions and dependence on non-renewable resources.

Future Challenges and Opportunities

Scaling Biotechnological Innovations

- Many bio-based innovations remain in the research and pilot phase, requiring investment in large-scale production facilities.
- Cost reductions through process optimization and economies of scale will be essential for commercial viability.

Regulatory and Public Acceptance

- Ensuring bioengineered products meet safety and environmental standards is critical for market adoption.
- Public awareness and consumer education will play a key role in promoting acceptance of bio-based innovations.

Role of AI and Automation in Optimizing Bio-Based Solutions

AI and automation are transforming the development, deployment, and optimization of bio-based solutions. By improving process efficiency, reducing waste, and accelerating scientific discovery, AI-driven technologies enhance the scalability and economic viability of bio-based innovations. These advancements support industries in lowering emissions, increasing resource efficiency, and integrating bio-based alternatives into mainstream markets.

AI for Research and Development in Bio-Based Solutions

Accelerating Biotechnological Innovation

- AI-driven computational modeling allows scientists to design and optimize genetically engineered crops, microorganisms, and enzymes for enhanced carbon sequestration and bio-based material production.
- Machine learning algorithms analyze vast datasets to predict the most efficient bioengineering pathways, reducing trial-and-error experimentation.

Optimizing Biofuel Production

- AI enhances fermentation processes by monitoring microbial activity in real time, adjusting environmental conditions to maximize biofuel yields.
- Predictive analytics improve feedstock selection, optimizing biomass conversion rates and reducing energy consumption in biorefineries.

Automation in Sustainable Agriculture and Land Management

Precision Farming for Carbon Sequestration

- Automated sensors and AI-powered drones monitor soil health, crop growth, and water usage, enabling data-driven decisions for sustainable agriculture.

- AI models predict optimal planting patterns and irrigation schedules to enhance carbon sequestration while maintaining high yields.

Robotics in Agroforestry and Reforestation

- Autonomous planting drones and robotic systems assist in large-scale reforestation efforts by efficiently distributing seeds and monitoring tree growth.
- AI-powered forest management tools analyze satellite imagery to detect deforestation risks and optimize conservation strategies.

AI in Circular Economy and Bio-Based Manufacturing

Waste-to-Resource Optimization

- AI-driven waste management systems identify and sort biodegradable materials, improving recycling efficiency for bio-based products.
- Automated biorefineries use machine learning to adjust processing conditions for maximum extraction of bio-based chemicals and fuels.

Enhancing Bioplastic and Sustainable Material Production

- AI algorithms predict material properties and optimize polymer formulations for biodegradable plastics, reducing production costs and improving performance.
- Automation in manufacturing facilities streamlines bio-based product development, reducing reliance on fossil-based materials.

Challenges and Future Prospects

Data Integration and Infrastructure Needs

- Expanding AI applications in bio-based industries requires robust data collection systems and advanced digital infrastructure.
- Cross-sector collaboration is essential to standardize data formats and improve interoperability between AI-driven platforms.

Ethical and Regulatory Considerations

- AI-driven bioengineering and automation must align with sustainability regulations and ethical guidelines to ensure responsible innovation.
- Transparent AI models and explainable decision-making processes will help gain public trust in bio-based technologies.

Future Policy Directions and International Collaboration

The large-scale adoption of bio-based solutions requires strong policy frameworks and coordinated international collaboration. As countries strive to meet climate goals and reduce emissions, aligning regulations, financial incentives, and cross-border initiatives will be critical to accelerating the transition to a bio-based economy. Future policy directions should focus on integrating bio-based solutions into climate strategies, enhancing funding mechanisms, and fostering global cooperation.

Strengthening Policy Frameworks for Bio-Based Solutions

Incorporating Bio-Based Solutions into Climate Strategies

- National climate policies, such as net-zero commitments and Nationally Determined Contributions (NDCs), should integrate bio-based innovations in sectors such as energy, agriculture, and manufacturing.

- Governments can establish clear targets for bio-based product adoption, similar to renewable energy mandates, to drive investment and industry transformation.

Standardizing Regulations and Sustainability Criteria

- Harmonizing sustainability standards for biofuels, bioplastics, and bio-based chemicals ensures consistency across markets and reduces regulatory uncertainty for businesses.
- Governments can introduce LCA requirements to assess the environmental impact of bio-based products and ensure they contribute to long-term sustainability.

Expanding Incentive Mechanisms

- Policies should provide financial incentives, such as tax credits, subsidies, and grants, to lower the cost barriers for bio-based industries.
- Carbon pricing mechanisms and emissions trading systems can be expanded to include bio-based carbon sequestration projects, such as soil carbon storage and reforestation.

Enhancing International Collaboration

Cross-Border Research and Innovation Partnerships

4. Collaborative research programs between governments, universities, and private sectors can accelerate technological advancements in bio-based materials, biofuels, and biotechnology.
5. Shared funding initiatives, such as international research grants, can support pilot projects and scale promising bio-based innovations.

Trade Agreements for Sustainable Bio-Based Products

- International trade agreements can include provisions that promote bio-based product adoption and remove trade barriers for sustainable materials.
- Mutual recognition of certification programs, such as sustainable biofuel standards, can create larger markets for bio-based alternatives.

Global Platforms for Policy Coordination

4. International organizations, such as the United Nations Framework Convention on Climate Change (UNFCCC) and the International Energy Agency (IEA), can facilitate policy alignment and best practice sharing.
5. Initiatives such as the Bioeconomy Council and public-private partnerships can help countries align policies and create a cohesive global bioeconomy strategy.

Challenges and Future Considerations

- Differences in national policies, regulatory frameworks, and economic priorities may create barriers to international alignment.
- Ensuring that bio-based solutions do not contribute to deforestation, food security concerns, or resource depletion requires strong governance mechanisms.
- Strengthening monitoring, reporting, and verification (MRV) systems will be crucial for tracking the impact of bio-based policies and ensuring accountability.

Breakthroughs and Disruptive Innovations

The rapid advancement of bio-based solutions is being driven by breakthroughs in biotechnology, materials science, and sustainable production methods. Disruptive innovations are reshaping industries by offering scalable alternatives to fossil-based products, improving carbon sequestration, and enhancing circular economy practices. These developments are making bio-based solutions more cost-effective, efficient, and widely applicable across sectors such as energy, agriculture, and manufacturing.

Next-Generation Bio-Based Materials

Precision-Engineered Biopolymers

- Advances in synthetic biology are enabling the development of high-performance biopolymers, such as PHA and PLA, which are biodegradable and derived from renewable sources.
- Innovations in enzyme engineering are improving the breakdown and recycling of bioplastics, reducing plastic waste and microplastic pollution.

Biofabrication and Mycelium-Based Materials

- Biofabrication techniques use microorganisms and fungi to create sustainable materials for textiles, construction, and packaging.
- Mycelium-based alternatives to leather, Styrofoam, and insulation are gaining traction as low-carbon, biodegradable substitutes for conventional materials.

Disruptive Technologies in Biofuels and Energy

Algae-Based Carbon Capture and Biofuel Production

- Engineered algae strains are improving the efficiency of biofuel production while simultaneously capturing CO_2 from industrial emissions.
- Algae-derived biofuels are emerging as viable replacements for aviation fuel, marine fuel, and other high-energy applications.

Electrofuels and Synthetic Biology for Energy

- Electrofuels (e-fuels) use renewable electricity and microbial processes to produce liquid biofuels with near-zero emissions.
- CRISPR-based gene editing is enhancing microbial pathways for more efficient biohydrogen and bioethanol production.

Carbon Sequestration and Climate Resilience Innovations

Engineered Soil Microbiomes

- Scientists are developing microbial inoculants that improve soil health, enhance nutrient uptake, and increase carbon sequestration in agricultural lands.
- Engineered bacteria can fix atmospheric nitrogen, reducing reliance on synthetic fertilizers and minimizing emissions.

Biochar for Carbon Storage and Soil Regeneration

- Pyrolysis technologies are advancing biochar production, creating carbon-negative soil amendments that improve water retention and nutrient cycling.
- Integrated biochar systems are being developed to capture emissions from agricultural and forestry waste streams.

Future Challenges and Adoption Pathways

Commercial Viability and Market Readiness

- Many disruptive bio-based technologies remain in early development or pilot phases, requiring investment and infrastructure for large-scale deployment.
- Reducing production costs through process optimization and economies of scale will be essential for market competitiveness.

Policy Support and Consumer Acceptance

- Regulatory frameworks must adapt to ensure new bio-based materials and fuels meet safety, sustainability, and performance standards.
- Consumer awareness and education will be critical in driving demand for disruptive bio-based innovations.

Conclusion

Bio-based solutions offer a transformative approach to reducing emissions, restoring ecosystems, and promoting sustainable land management. Throughout this book, we have explored the science behind bio-based strategies, their role in emissions reduction, and their potential for large-scale implementation across industries. Advances in bio-based technologies, such as bioplastics, biofuels, and carbon sequestration methods, demonstrate the feasibility of transitioning away from fossil-based systems.

Despite their benefits, the adoption of bio-based solutions faces challenges, including high production costs, regulatory uncertainties, and infrastructure limitations. Addressing these barriers requires policy support, financial incentives, and collaborative efforts among governments, industries, and research institutions. Measuring the impact of bio-based innovations through tools like LCA and remote sensing ensures accountability and effectiveness.

The future of bio-based climate action depends on the integration of emerging technologies, such as synthetic biology, AI, and automation. These innovations will enhance efficiency, reduce costs, and accelerate the transition toward circular bioeconomy models. Strengthening international collaboration, aligning policies, and expanding investment in bio-based industries will be critical to scaling these solutions and maximizing their long-term impact.

Call to Action for Scaling Bio-Based Solutions

To realize the full potential of bio-based solutions, stakeholders must take proactive steps in research, investment, and policy development. Governments should implement clear regulatory frameworks that incentivize bio-based industries, establish sustainability standards, and integrate these solutions into national climate strategies. Expanding green financing mechanisms, such as carbon pricing, tax incentives, and public-private partnerships, will encourage businesses to adopt bio-based alternatives.

Industries must prioritize sustainable production practices by investing in bio-based technologies and transitioning supply chains toward renewable resources. Companies can contribute by integrating bio-based materials into manufacturing, adopting circular economy principles, and participating in emissions reduction initiatives.

Research institutions and innovators play a key role in advancing bio-based solutions by improving efficiency, scalability, and sustainability. Collaborative efforts between academia and industry will accelerate the commercialization of bio-based innovations, making them more accessible and cost-effective. Public awareness campaigns and education initiatives can further drive consumer demand and market growth for bio-based products.

By aligning policy, industry, and research efforts, bio-based solutions can be effectively scaled to address climate change, resource depletion, and environmental degradation.

Closing Thoughts on Long-Term Sustainability

The transition to a bio-based economy represents a crucial step toward long-term sustainability. By harnessing nature-based solutions, technological advancements, and policy alignment, we can create resilient, low-carbon systems that support both economic growth and environmental health. Bio-based solutions are not a temporary fix but a fundamental shift toward a sustainable future. As global challenges intensify, investing in bio-based innovations will be essential to ensuring climate resilience, ecosystem restoration, and resource security for future generations. The time to act is now—scaling bio-based solutions will define our collective ability to build a more sustainable and regenerative world.

www.ingramcontent.com/pod-product-compliance
Lightning Source LLC
Chambersburg PA
CBHW052139270326
41930CB00012B/2943